The Joys of Jennifer

Finding Success for Your Child with CHARGE Syndrome or Other Challenges

Written by
Carolyn Siewicki

FERNE PRESS

The Joys of Jennifer: Finding Success for Your Child with CHARGE Syndrome or Other Challenges

Copyright © 2013 by Carolyn Siewicki
Layout and cover design by Jacqueline L. Challiss Hill
Printed in the United States of America
Cover Photo © Carlosphotos | Dreamstime.com

Summary: A parent shows how her child thrived when doctors told her it was not possible.

Library of Congress Cataloging-in-Publication Data
    Siewicki, Carolyn
    The Joys of Jennifer: Finding Success for Your Child with CHARGE Syndrome
    or Other Challenges/Carolyn Siewicki–First Edition
    ISBN-13: 978-19-38326-21-9
    1. Non-fiction. 2. CHARGE. 3. Parenting a child with a disability.
    I. Siewicki, Carolyn II. Title
    Library of Congress Control Number: 2013939127

A portion of the proceeds from the sale of this book will be given to The CHARGE Syndrome Foundation, The Pulmonary Hypertension Research Center at New York-Presbyterian/Morgan Stanley Children's Hospital, New York, and Make-A-Wish Foundation of Michigan.

FERNE PRESS

Ferne Press is an imprint of Nelson Publishing & Marketing
366 Welch Road, Northville, MI 48167
www.nelsonpublishingandmarketing.com
(248) 735-0418

Dedication

This book is dedicated to our beautiful daughter, Jennifer, who has given us so much joy in our lives. She really knows how to live life to the fullest. We thank God for giving her to us.

Larry, Jennifer, and I want to acknowledge:
Our sons, Matthew and Christopher, their wives, Shera and Gemina, and Jennifer's Grandma Loncharich, who have always been there for us.

Our friends and family for their support, love, interest, and inclusion in their lives. Jennifer's friends who have never forgotten her and enjoy her joyful spirit.

The Arc of Northwest Wayne County for always directing us to a resource when called upon.

Sylvan Learning Center for giving Jennifer her first job.

The staff and professors at Oakland University and Madonna University for giving Jennifer one of the best gifts of total acknowledgment of her as a person.

All the individuals who have worked with, volunteered with, and given Jennifer a chance in her life to become a better person.

My publisher, Marian Nelson, and editor, Kris Yankee, for making this project a reality.

Chapter One

I am the mother of a daughter who shouldn't have lived. "She has large black spaces in her brain. She will be severely mentally impaired. She won't be able to think or accomplish much of anything. Her head is small and has microcephaly." Those were the words the doctor said to me and my husband about our very sick newborn.

My husband, Larry, responded by asking if they could be wrong. Maybe the black spaces would fill in with time as she grows.

"No" was their reply.

We would not believe what we were told. Jennifer fought too hard this first month of her life to live. We knew they could be wrong. She responded to our touch; her heart rate would go up on the monitors. How could she respond like that if nothing was going on in her brain?

We walked to our vehicle, silent and in shock, after hearing this news. Why in the world wouldn't the doctors give us any hope? That should be medical school 101—always give a glimmer of hope even when things appear hopeless.

Our feelings those first four months of Jennifer's hospitalization were similar in many ways, but also very different. I was more guarded about her condition and felt numbness. We both felt that the best thing for Jennifer was to get her home to her family where she would get better. While Jennifer was in the hospital, fighting for her life, I didn't know if she would make it, but Larry always felt she would. It seemed that every day the doctors told us more bad news.

If I could go back to that time, this is what I'd ask the doctors: why would you send her home at two months old with such labored breathing that her little chest would heave up and down so dramatically?

I trusted the doctors, but it didn't take me long to know they sent her home to die.

So to all the doctors who said she wouldn't think or accomplish anything, I submit the following:

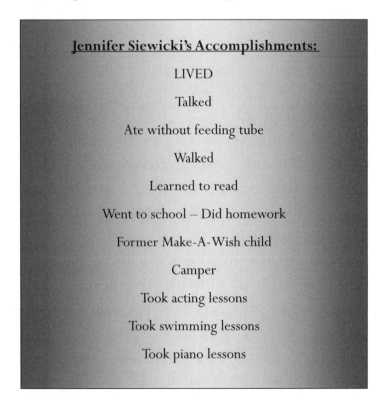

Jennifer Siewicki's Accomplishments:

LIVED

Talked

Ate without feeding tube

Walked

Learned to read

Went to school – Did homework

Former Make-A-Wish child

Camper

Took acting lessons

Took swimming lessons

Took piano lessons

Took violin lessons

Took karate lessons and earned a yellow belt

Boater

Baseball team player

Soccer team player

Did homework in high school

Graduated high school with a diploma

Held a job

Attended Madonna University
where she audited two media classes

Volunteered at Make-A-Wish

Attended television production certification training

Received driver's permit

Drove 6-speed Corvette she won from Make-A-Wish

Volunteered at Livonia Jaycees

Attended three-day actors' workshop

Attended Schoolcraft College (online classes)

Attended Oakland University (OU) for three years
and received certificate of completion

Lived on her own in an apartment for three years
when she went to OU

Used scooter to navigate around campus at OU

Member of sorority at OU

DJ of own radio show at OU—WXOU

Volunteered at Michigan Humane Society

Performed her own parodies at karaoke venues

<u>Ongoing accomplishments:</u>

Harley-Davidson passenger rider (went to Bike Week in Myrtle Beach, SC, in H. D. sidecar motorcycle)

Riding in Harley-Davidson sidecar with Mom and Dad.

Volunteers at OU Film Camp during summers

Bicycle riding with PEAC (Programs to Educate All Cyclists)

Horseback riding lessons

Downhill skiing

Kayaking

Waterskiing

Fishing

Writing stories/parodies

Making movies

Member of Detroit Puppeteers Guild

Member of Dr. Paws Pet Therapy

Volunteers at Project Linus making blankets for hospitals

Volunteers weekly at Friends of MI Animal Rescue
in Belleville, MI

Looking for job, fills out applications, and has interviews

Using public transportation

Applying for jobs online and out of state–Hollywood
and New York

Navigating sites on computer

Awards

May, 2007: Received award for self-determination from
The Arc of Northwest Wayne County, MI

As you can see, the infant who went home to die has lived to accomplish what we were told would never happen. Our story is one of hope, strength, and faith.

Chapter Two

In the later months of my pregnancy, I had a feeling that something was just not right. The baby was quiet in the womb, not moving much at all. I never shared my feelings, not even with Larry. Maybe I thought that if I said something out loud, it would become a real possibility of something bad happening. A lot of people say they don't care what the sex of the baby is as long as it's healthy, but until you've lived through life with a sick baby, you couldn't possibly know *how* meaningful those words are.

A mother's first instinct
is to blame herself if her child is not perfect;
be careful to not do this.

Three weeks before the baby was due, I was putting freshly washed baby clothes in the dresser. I went to bed and at four o'clock in the morning, my water broke. I called the doctor and he said to rest until the office opened. I called my mom to come over to stay with my two boys, and we went to St. Mary's Hospital in Livonia, Michigan.

Jennifer was born at 12:31 p.m. by C-section. She was five pounds and eighteen inches long. She had the cord wrapped once around her neck, was blue, and didn't cry. The doctor and nurses tried suctioning out her nasal passages, but it wasn't working at all. They were able to suction through her mouth, and then they gave Jennifer oxygen. My husband was with me and everyone in the operating room didn't want me upset, so they downplayed the critical situation. They whisked the baby out of the room, with Larry following. Larry watched while the pediatrician tried to get an IV in the baby's head without success. His heart broke watching Jennifer in pain. I was later told that the Neonatal Intensive Care Unit (NICU) team from Detroit Children's Hospital was called in to help. Their team was able to place the IV in Jennifer's head and to stabilize her.

A nurse asked Larry if he wanted the baby baptized and he said yes. He remembers running behind a small nurse, her little legs moving swiftly. The priest from the hospital gave the baby "the last rites" and baptized her Jennifer Henrietta Siewicki. Larry said that at the moment she was baptized, a glow appeared around her and she started doing better. It was the first of several miracles to happen.

Larry didn't know what he was going to say to me about our baby when I was in recovery. At that point, I hadn't realized the seriousness of the situation and was more concerned about her being baptized with Henrietta as her middle name. I wasn't sure this was the name I wanted for her. Before this, we had not made a final decision. We wanted her middle name to be after my dad, Henry, and Henrietta was what we came up with. Her birth certificate reads Jennifer H. Siewicki, a compromise to Henrietta. Now I would have had her middle name read Henry. My dad was an outstanding man and father, and I wanted to honor him. Jennifer certainly reflects his strength and courage, then as an infant and to this day as an adult.

After Jennifer was stabilized by the NICU team from Children's, she was brought to my room so I could see her. She was in an incubator right next to my bed. I could put my hand through the holes and touch her. I had to lie flat on my back because of the medication I was given during delivery. I remember her being quiet and resting peacefully while the nurse used an Ambu bag over her nose and mouth to make her breathe.

I was sad because Jennifer was very sick and she couldn't come home with me. I thought that with her in the hospital for maybe a week she would come home to her family, but that was not to be.

Jennifer was taken to Children's Hospital in Detroit and placed in the NICU. I spoke with the doctors constantly from my bed at St. Mary's Hospital. It was too early to tell me much, but they did find out that she had a blockage in her nasal passages that her Ear, Nose, and Throat (ENT) doctor had to correct through surgery.

Larry brought her brothers to the hospital. They were not allowed in the NICU, but the nurse brought her incubator to the window so they could see her. Matthew was eight years old and Christopher was four years old. Matthew recalls that even though he didn't understand the extent of Jennifer's issues, he realized that she was small and struggling. Both he and Christopher were very excited to see their new baby sister.

Larry went to be with Jennifer when the doctors needed to put a central IV line in her chest. The central IV line was used for medications and fluids. They felt it would be easier on her than trying to keep finding a vein each time. She was put on a ventilator for two weeks and with oxygen. Back then they would have to poke her little finger to measure the oxygen in her blood. She sure had a lot of marks on her from all the poking.

I went straight to Children's Hospital when I was discharged. We had to scrub, put sanitary gowns on over our clothes and booties over our shoes. I didn't hold her until she was off the ventilator. Even then I didn't want to hold her much because I just wanted her to rest and not be disturbed. I used to go in the mornings to visit her after I got Matthew off to school and Christopher to a friend's. Some days I wouldn't even get to be with her because the doctors would do rounds in the morning. They would attend to all the babies in the unit and I would have to wait. I didn't want to take advantage of people watching the boys too long. Larry would visit Jennifer every day after work. One time, he took a friend with him and told the staff he was "Uncle Mike" so they would let him in. It did mean a lot to Larry and me.

Jennifer used to turn blue when she was a newborn, but nobody knew exactly why. I knew she was feisty even as an infant, and that was confirmed when a doctor called me and told me he couldn't do some testing because he said, "Jennifer was an uncooperative patient."

Within the first two months, while Jennifer was still in the hospital, the doctors noticed that one eye was remaining partly opened. Her face showed the signs of facial palsy and when the pediatrician told me about it, he genuinely felt bad. He had a very serious look on his face every time he broke more and more bad news to us about Jennifer. Larry and I both felt sorry for her pediatricians because they constantly had to be the messengers of bad news to this little baby's parents. We could see the stress on their faces and hear it in their voices. Usually I was the one who was told any information, and then I had to call my husband at work and cry to him about yet another turn of events.

After the doctor told us about the facial palsy, I would drive past signs along the highway and see a picture of a pretty girl. I would try to imagine Jennifer's face as she got older with one side droopy. I would look in the mirror and try to scrunch up one side of my face and keep the other side from moving so I could imagine what she might look like. Of course it saddened us. Jennifer's ENT doctor told us that when Jennifer was older, she could make a decision to have what would be like a facelift to correct the facial palsy. She would have to exercise her facial muscles to get away from the droopiness of her right side.

Next, the doctors told us Jennifer had black spaces in her brain which shouldn't be there. Of course this was very upsetting to us. When we left the hospital, Larry escorted me to my car which I had parked on the street. When we approached the vehicle, we noticed that someone had tried to break in but was unsuccessful driving off. We asked security to help us get the car started and when all was done, we actually laughed and laughed. Like, are you kidding me? Could this day get any worse? It really was a tension reliever.

After two long months of Jennifer staying in the NICU, we were told she could come home. When Jennifer was hospitalized for so long, I remember covering her crib with a sheet because it was too painful to look at it. She should've been with me.

A few days before Jennifer was to come home, we went out on a lake as a family with our boat. For me it was not to have a fun-filled day at the lake, but much more. I was so scared and nervous about her homecoming that I needed to settle myself down and regroup. Just sitting quietly on the water was very tranquil for me. I also knew it would be a long time before our family would be able to do something like that again.

The day Jennifer was released, my parents stayed at our house with the boys. They were very excited to have their sister home, just as we were.

We arrived at the hospital early that morning. The hospital gave us a start-up supply of items that we would need for Jennifer's tube feedings. We had been trained the previous weeks to tube feed her. I was nervous to bring her home. She was so fragile and small. She didn't suck, so she had to be tube fed through the mouth every two hours. Since the doctors must've felt I could take care of her, I figured I could do it, too.

It felt very chaotic when we came home that day. Family and friends were there. The oxygen company came to bring a portable tank and supplies in case Jennifer needed oxygen. Our emotions were high. We were very, very happy to finally be bringing our baby home.

My youngest son's fifth birthday was that weekend and we debated on having the family birthday party as we normally did. My dad was against it because he felt it would be too much commotion for the baby. We gave it a lot of thought and decided to go ahead with it because we wanted to maintain as much normalcy as possible in our household. Not only did the family get to celebrate my son's birthday, but they were able to meet Jennifer.

During those first few days at home, the visiting nurse came over and gave us a quick CPR lesson. She was scheduled to come back the next day when there was more time to give a more lengthy lesson. The visiting nurse was obviously unnerved when she asked us if we had been taught CPR. We had not. I wanted to question her about why a social worker hadn't been assigned to our case. I never saw one. I knew the other NICU babies' parents were seeing one. I remember passing by the social workers' office door thinking that I should knock and meet with one, but I didn't. I was scared. But now my thought is shame on all of the doctors; they could have at least given her a chance for life.

When Jennifer stopped breathing, we went into action performing CPR as the nurse had taught us. After reviving Jennifer, we drove her to the nearest hospital, but the doctors didn't know what to do with her and told us to drive to Children's Hospital in Detroit. How could you send a little fragile baby on her way without putting her in an ambulance? Are you kidding me? She almost died, for gosh sakes! Even our son Christopher remembers being afraid when she turned blue. He was so scared and confused.

Jennifer was immediately put into the Pediatric Intensive Care Unit (PICU). She couldn't go back into the NICU because she had left the hospital. The decision was made to perform a tracheotomy to ease her labored breathing. She looked so tiny in what appeared to be a large room with monitors all around her. Her heart rate kept dropping, so she was prescribed medication to regulate it. The hospital did a sleep study on her to rule out SIDS. I kept myself together until some nurses from the NICU came to see us and asked how we were doing. I fell apart for the first time but I quickly regrouped, ready to face what was next.

It seemed every day Jennifer had some sort of setback. We began to face each day with a kind of numbness, trying to absorb it all. It was then that I found out what the word "surreal" meant. I lived in a daze. A person can only cry so much. At one point, I spoke with a minister at the hospital expressing my guilt about silently planning my daughter's funeral and how my husband was just the opposite, never having those thoughts, always believing. The minister eased my worries by explaining that our feelings balanced each other's out.

Allow yourself to grieve for the baby you didn't have.

We had heard about some monies available for parents who needed help caring for their medically fragile babies. A team of people evaluated our little four-month-old baby who was still in the hospital struggling to survive and actually told us we were rejected because she was on so many medications that they did not feel they could accurately evaluate her. We were stunned. That money was available to parents like us to bring their struggling babies home. I really believe they didn't think she would make it and didn't want to "waste" the money. What else could have been the real reason for that ridiculous decision?

We looked into our insurance. It did have a provision to provide twenty-four-hour nursing care, but they would pay half and we would be responsible for the other half. I called anyone who would listen to my problem until I eventually ran out of people to call. I threw my pen down and said, "God, it's in your hands. I can't do anything more." The next day I received a return call from one of the nursing agencies I had contacted, requesting they waive the other 50% payment that I would have been responsible for, and they agreed.

I remember running down my street to tell anyone that was outside my wonderful news. Jennifer was finally coming home. Another MIRACLE!

And another day later, I received a call that another agency would help me if I still needed help. I remember asking them, "So you're saying you would provide services to help me bring my baby home?" and the woman said *"Yes."*

Jennifer had maintained her birth weight and was stabilized enough to come home after another two months. She wasn't what I'd call "better," but rather stable. After we were given training on suctioning the trach, our beautiful baby with the crooked smile (a nurse once said "a face only a mother could love") came home by the end of August. By Christmas of that year, she was starting to thrive. She had been diagnosed with failure to thrive while in the hospital.

The next three years consisted of 24/7 nursing services. They were the most difficult of all the years, not knowing if your baby would survive and having all sorts of people in your home constantly. From therapists, early intervention schooling in the home, to nurses and delivery people for her hospital supplies, we were never alone.

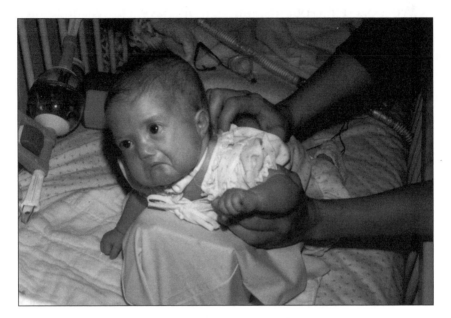

Jennifer's home therapy.

*Find others who will love your child
as much as you do.*

Sometimes the shift-change nurse wouldn't show up and one of us would cover the shift. There were several middle-of-the-night shifts that Larry or I took on and didn't sleep the next day because that day was another working day for us, with Larry going to work and me being home with the kids. I had to be on few of the nurses much of the time. One would tend to fall asleep in the rocker while Jennifer was resting in a bouncer next to her (she would have to be in a semi-upright position in case she would vomit). I would constantly be in and out of the room keeping the nurse up. If I had to go out, I would call several times to make sure the nurse was awake for my baby.

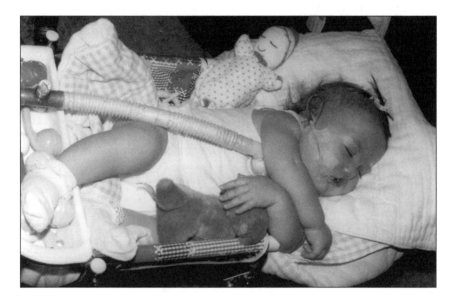

Jennifer struggling to survive.

That same nurse did love Jennifer and was really good with her when Jennifer and she were awake. People might say, "Just get rid of her," but believe me, it wasn't that easy. There were only so many nurses available at the agency and there were all sorts of personality issues. Eventually I did let this particular nurse go, but for other reasons.

Another nurse drew up one of Jennifer's medications when she was only five pounds and I noticed the syringe with the green medicine in it. It looked like a lot so I checked it out before she put it in the feeding tube and sure enough it was drawn at 2 cc's instead of .02 cc's, which is a **big** difference, especially for such a small baby! The medicine was a heart medication and I believe that too much could have killed Jennifer. It was a miracle I even noticed.

The way we were living was exhausting. There was so much to do to take care of our medically fragile baby and spend some time with our other children. But we were still young and had energy. Jennifer was our child whom we loved very much, our responsibility, and we cared for her the best we could, as well as making time for our sons. Usually we divided up our time with them so one of us was still with Jennifer. Larry would take them on weekend camping trips occasionally with his brother and nephew. They would go on the boat to Lake Erie to fish with the guys. I would take them to their soccer games and practices. I feel we did a great job juggling our lives.

Chapter Three

As Jennifer was getting older, she became stronger and bigger. She had lots of personality. She was so funny, even as a baby. She had these chubby cheeks and sparkling blue eyes and a big grin that wouldn't quit. She was like my two other kids, except for the medical problems.

Our son Matthew said that Jennifer had that spark about her that made him happy, made him want to be with her. She always brought a lot of joy. It made him feel good to be around her. She was always entertaining.

The neurologist said Jennifer would never talk, but Jennifer did. She used to put her tiny, tiny finger in her trach and say little sentences. The doctor did acknowledge her talking and said doctors can be wrong and he was glad he was.

Since birth, Jennifer had been orally fed through a tube. Around two and a half years old, she began chewing on the tube. At a doctor's visit, we discussed putting the tube in her stomach and we set up the surgery. We told Jennifer that if she could swallow food without the feeding tube, she wouldn't need the surgery. During the summer of 1987, I would bring her high chair outside and we would watch her brothers and friends swim in our pool while she tried, without fussing, to eat without the tube. Jennifer was fed for two-hour stretches at a time. Eat some, throw up, clean up, and eat some more until she was getting more in than she was throwing up. She never gave up trying. Even as a youngster, I would describe Jennifer as having determination, strength, and a desire to please her mother. What a feeling it was to call the doctor and tell him Jennifer was eating on her own and to cancel the surgery.

Also that summer, the ENT doctor scheduled a surgery to put a scope down her esophagus to check on her bronchial pulmonary dysplasia, which had been brought on by ventilator use during infancy. When we were checking in at the hospital, I saw on the paperwork D-Canalization, which meant to take out the trach, so I was puzzled but hopeful that her trach would come out. D-Canalization had been tried before during these scopings, but Jennifer's body hadn't been ready.

Sure enough when we saw her in recovery, her trach tube was hanging on the side of the crib. That was a great day. Now we could move forward with our lives, just Larry, me, and the kids. That was the end of the need for nursing services and a return to a somewhat normal life for our family.

Jennifer also began walking that same summer. We had always practiced, but she just couldn't get it. We had one doctor at Children's Hospital who usually had at least a two-hour wait, so she practiced walking the halls. For some reason the narrowness of the hallways seemed to help her feel safe. I'm not sure if that was the truth, but that is actually when she started walking. From there it was practice, practice, and more practice, always with enthusiasm and a smile. Even with all the falls.

Look for the good in everything about your child.

Jennifer was signed up to begin preschool that September. I went to the school in the summer and explained the changes Jennifer had gone through over the last few months of eating, walking, and no longer having the trach tube. We had to meet with staff and make a new plan for Jennifer because she had accomplished a lot since our last meeting. An IEP (individual educational plan) was drafted for her first year of preschool. IEPs are educational goals set for each school year for students with a disability in special education and are made specifically for the student's individual needs.

She went to preschool for two years and it was amazing. I used to drive her because I didn't want her to take a bus. Her first three years of life had been really tough and she wasn't ready to take a bus. There were probably six students in her class with a teacher and a paraprofessional. Jennifer went in the mornings. The students would sit in a group for class work, have a snack, go for walks in a nearby park, and do various projects.

Fortunately, Jennifer had some previous interaction with other children. She had not only her brothers but a lot of neighbor children. The little girls in the neighborhood loved being with Jennifer.

At the end of two years in preschool, there was a graduation party. It was so cute! Jennifer let me put her hair in pigtails, which she usually hated me to do probably because of the IVs in her head that she had to endure in infancy. My son can still remember when the students were lined up sitting in chairs at graduation. Jennifer was in a beautiful dress and she wiggled her foot over to a little boy's foot and very nonchalantly stepped down. We didn't even know Jennifer could even think of pranks and be "bad." We actually laughed about it and were glad she didn't hurt the boy.

Our first family vacation was for four days at Torch Lake, Michigan, over the 4th of July when Jennifer was five years old. We had a 19' Bayliner, named Jennifer II, which we hauled to the Chain of Lakes. We were all very excited to go as a family of five. With Larry having his own business, it was really, really difficult for him to get away from the shop. He always worked at least fifteen hours a day, six days a week. This was a luxury to have us all together.

Because we didn't know if Jennifer would get sick or if Larry could get away from work, we didn't make reservations for our trip. The first night it was getting late, but we managed to find a room on Torch Lake in a small motel. It was pretty small for the five of us, but we squeezed in. Nobody complained. We were just happy to be together.

The next day, we drove to Clam Lake and found a beautiful condo on the lake. We were set for the rest of our trip. We were acting like a real family.

There is something soothing about the water. I've always found it very therapeutic. We boated, fished, and enjoyed the time together, although I remember Larry didn't really feel re-laxed until the ride home because he worried about his shop.

He was pretty stressed and quiet until the end. We did have a great time, though. I remember looking for a nearby hospital in the area in case Jennifer ran into trouble, but fortunately we didn't need one. She was great and was so cute in her little Mickey Mouse bathing suit.

First family vacation.

When we were on Clam Lake we stopped the boat so the children could see the beautiful swans, but that proved to be a mistake. The swans started racing toward our boat and honking loudly. They must have felt threatened and we didn't waste any time speeding away. There was a restaurant we went to on Torch Lake that boaters could pull right up to and have a meal on the outside deck. There were rubber ducky races on Bellaire Lake on the 4th of July. It was a blast.

Although there was some anxiety involved, worries about Jennifer and if she could handle a vacation or would she have some sort of emergency, the trip was beautiful.

After preschool Jennifer went to a special education self-contained classroom in a neighborhood elementary school. The bus ride was an hour, and with her physical condition, in hot weather, it was way too long. I started my phone calls to the Board of Education office until I reached the top of the "ladder" and finally, Jennifer received permission to ride in a cab at no expense to us.

Kindergarten was wonderful for Jennifer. She made a lot of friends and was very happy. When Jennifer was happy, mama was happy. It was a great school year. She did get a lot of respiratory infections that first year, but the doctor said as she got older that would get better, and he was right. The only bad thing to happen during that year was our New York trip and her final diagnosis, but as far as school went, it was wonderful.

Chapter Four

At one of Jennifer's cardiologist visits, she'd had an echocardiogram. The results showed high pressures in the pulmonary artery and an enlarged right side of her heart. This information led to the necessity of a heart catheterization. Jennifer was diagnosed with pulmonary hypertension (PH) at Children's Hospital in Detroit after the heart catheterization in January 1989. We were told, once again, to take her home and enjoy her because there was nothing they could do. Again, we couldn't accept that. It was before the Internet, so there was not much information available and even harder to find anything out. We spoke to a lot of different people about our situation.

My sister-in-law, who lives in Pennsylvania, spoke to her girlfriend about Jennifer's diagnosis. Her friend was a nurse to a cardiologist in New York City, who then spoke to the doctor. We were informed about a cardiologist in our area who studied under a cardiologist at Columbia Presbyterian Hospital in NYC, which was the only research center in the world at the time for pulmonary hypertension. We immediately contacted the local doctor. We met with the doctor and he made the referral to the director of PH at Babies and Children's Hospital, Columbia Presbyterian. In April 1989, we borrowed a car and money from my parents. They took care of our boys while we were gone for over a week in NYC for testing.

The head nurse gave us all the information we needed for a place to stay, parking, and the restaurants around town. As for the restaurants, our meals consisted of bagels with cream cheese and coffee from the vendors on the streets because we were so very busy with all the tests. I think one time we ate in the cafeteria in the hospital. We would rather have eaten from the street vendors.

We made the twelve-hour trip in one day. We didn't realize that the sun went down earlier on the East Coast, so we were trying to beat the clock when we were nearing the city. We needed to find our place before it got dark. It was difficult enough driving in the city during daylight hours. The traffic was unbelievable. We were scared being in a strange town, a strange hospital, not knowing what to expect.

At the very first light in the city just over the George Washington Bridge, we had a couple of people trying to wash our front window for money. We soon learned that if you turn your wipers on they know you do not want your windows washed. There were a lot of one-way streets, but after a few bad turns, we finally found the rooming house that the hospital used for patients' families. There was no Ronald McDonald House there. We had to triple park at a very, very old building a couple blocks from the hospital. We buzzed and a caretaker, who was expecting us, let us in. The rooming house had a room with a sink, but the whole floor shared a bathroom and kitchen. It was the scariest place I've ever stayed.

The next morning, we went to the hospital where Jennifer and I stayed for a week. Larry went back and forth to the rooming house. I was too scared to stay at the rooming house alone. I would sleep on a cot next to Jennifer. We were in a research lab room with five patient beds crammed almost on top of each other and with only enough room for one parent for each child to squeeze next to. Larry would bring me a change of clothes every day and I would shower at the hospital.

Even though we were in an older, rougher area of NYC—a shooting had taken place at a bank across the street while we were there, and farther down the block we were told was where Malcolm X had been killed—I do have to say that the people of New York City are very kind to people with challenges. From the street vendor giving Jennifer a free donut to the restaurant owner giving her whatever she wanted to eat, time and again the people of NYC showed their gentler side to our girl. They earned our respect.

Each day was filled with tests. Every morning they would give us a stack of slips for tests. When the slips were gone, you were done for the day. It was very tiring for all of us but especially for Jennifer who wasn't quite five years old yet. We barely could eat lunch. One time we tried to sneak in a hot dog from a vendor and eat it in the hospital lobby when our nurse saw us from the second floor and yelled down to hurry up, they were waiting for us. That's pretty much how it was all week.

We didn't know what the doctor was going to tell us and what the results from all the tests would be. When they did Jennifer's blood tests, we were asked to go to the cashier's office where we were told that they wanted $4,000 for blood work. I could barely speak but called the nurse right away and she came right down. She explained to the cashier's office to bill the research center. We were very relieved about that. For one test, Jennifer was injected with a dye and then scanned. For most of the tests, she wasn't allowed to move. She was an angel. She was the best. For another test she had to drink a radioactive substance, have a machine that covered her whole body come just a fraction of an inch from her face, and not move for an hour. Larry and I would take turns telling her stories to help her lay still.

By the end of the week, the doctor prescribed Coumadin to keep her blood thin to prevent clots in her lungs, and he also prescribed oxygen for the night. When Jennifer sleeps, her blood oxygen level goes down very low. There were no other kinds of medicine to prescribe for PH at that time. But with Jennifer being so young and with mild symptoms, she had time for technology to catch up.

On the way home, we stopped at my sister-in-law's and brother-in-law's house in Pennsylvania for a short visit and a chance to regroup. This was what we usually did when we went to our appointments in NYC. My in-laws were always so hospitable and welcomed us into their home even with having a large family of four children of their own. We really appreciated their hospitality. That's what families do for each other.

That was the first of many of our trips to NYC, even to this day. We had gone as many as four times a year to once every other year depending on what new drug was out and how Jennifer was doing. Jennifer saw a local doctor when we didn't travel to New York for a checkup and a few tests. Now there is a PH center at the University of Michigan Hospital where Jennifer sees her doctor.

During one of Jennifer's early New York hospital visits, a geneticist walked into Jennifer's room, took one look at her, and diagnosed her with CHARGE Association (an acronym for a rare disorder). We were never told in Michigan why she was the way she was other than she was just born that way. Obviously, the doctors in Michigan didn't know about CHARGE. We were actually very happy to have a name to why she had so many congenital abnormalities. He said it was because of her features that led him to that conclusion. We were told to contact NORD (National Organization for Rare Disorders) for more information. I did, but because I already had so much to deal with with Jennifer's very serious disease of pulmonary hypertension, I did not pursue it. All we knew was that we had to deal with her immediate problems.

Chapter Five

We were unsure what the CHARGE symptoms were, but over the years we have found that there are several that make up the acronym. Not all symptoms need to be present in the patient for the diagnosis to be CHARGE, as you can see by the symptoms that Jennifer does and does not exhibit. They are as follows:

Could Have:	Jennifer
C-Coloboma of the eye (a condition where normal tissue in and around the eye is missing at birth)	No
H-Heart defects	Yes
A-Atresia of choanae (a condition where the nasal passages don't form correctly)	Yes
R-Retardation (delay) of growth and/or development	Yes
G-Genital and/or urinary abnormalities	No
E-Ear abnormalities and deafness	Yes

When Jennifer was born, she did not have the diagnosis of CHARGE, most likely because it was so rare. All her different problems were called "congenital abnormalities," which to me just meant birth defects.

She was diagnosed with bronchopulmonary dysplasia (BPD). With the diagnosis of having BPD, the atresia of the choanae and small airways, Jennifer had trouble breathing. Her chest would move up and down heavily with labored breathing until she had a trach put in at two months old. We have now discovered that getting a tracheotomy seems to be a typical occurrence in CHARGE children. Cleft lip and palate occur sometimes in CHARGE patients, but Jennifer doesn't have these. Gastroesophageal reflux disease occurs with CHARGE, but it never was really established that Jennifer had reflux. She did have projectile vomiting often.

Jennifer does have heart defects. She did have atresia of choanae at birth, which was repaired within a day or two. Babies naturally breathe through their noses and Jennifer had this blockage and so could not. She does have the delay of growth and of development. She does not have genital or urinary abnormalities.

Jennifer's heart, a cardiologist told us, was enlarged on the right side, but he wasn't too concerned. We never knew she had two holes in her heart until we had Jennifer seen at New York Columbia Presbyterian Hospital in New York City. Jennifer turned blue when she was stressed sometimes, but in those early years the doctors did not know why. Later, at Jennifer's hospital visit in New York City, we were told her heart shunted from right to left (the blood would sometimes seep through the hole in her heart) and the blood mixed with the oxygenated blood and that was why she turned blue. She was diagnosed with pulmonary hypertension, which is not part of CHARGE.

In regards to Jennifer's hearing and the shape of her ears, I could see as a newborn that the shape looked different, but until the geneticist told us about CHARGE, we just attributed it to a congenital abnormality. I felt that it was the least of her problems. I did notice that Jennifer favored her right side to hear as a baby. At that time, we did not know she had a hearing loss. Jennifer probably did not get her hearing aids until she was around three years old. Even though she has profound hearing loss in her left ear, she still had a hearing aid just in case it may have helped. It wasn't until after high school that the doctor said the left hearing aid didn't make much of a difference in her hearing. Now she just wears one in the right side. It's an in-the-ear aid. She had a pair that went around the ear but they ALWAYS flopped around because of the shape of her ears from CHARGE. When she was little and going to school, I would use strings that you would normally put eyeglasses on for her hearing aids and pin them to the back of her shirt. That way, if they fell out of her ear they would not be lost. Jennifer always wanted a little, itty bitty aid, but because of her hearing loss and the structure of her ear, she could not get the smaller aid. She actually hears really, really well with the use of her aid. She is very good at taking care of it and only takes it out for showers and bedtime. The first thing she does in the morning is put in her hearing aid. She loves it.

When we flew to Las Vegas for her 21st birthday, her hearing aid stopped working. She was very upset because she couldn't hear. Our friends somehow found a pharmacy and bought new batteries, but that wasn't the problem with it. After talking to her audiologist we think the flight may have had something to do with the digital hearing aid not working. Now Jennifer carries a spare aid and batteries with her in her purse at all times.

Jennifer does not have coloboma of the eyes, but she did have issues with her eyes. Whether or not this issue is because of CHARGE, we don't know. She did have surgery a couple times for blocked tear ducts as a baby. She wore an eye patch for a few years beginning at about two years old on her left eye, several hours a day, to strengthen her right eye. The eye doctor said if she didn't wear it, she would lose the vision in that eye. It wasn't the easiest thing in the world to do. She would usually scrunch the eye patch up in a little ball with her tiny hand and rip it off. If we could salvage it, we would tape it back on with a skin tape and reuse it for that day. I would give her a little break before putting it back on her. It was especially difficult when it was hot out and she would be sweating. I'm sure it was uncomfortable for her. We would try to put it on her early in the day. Her vision is not the best in the right eye, but with glasses and the good vision in her left eye, she does just fine.

Low muscle tone is a characteristic of CHARGE. Her muscle tone was low as a newborn. She had occupational therapy and physical therapy as soon as she came home from the hospital at four months old. Crawling, sitting, and walking were all delayed. Her gait was always wide and she kept her arms raised a bit for balance. When she got a tricycle, it was too hard for her to get the pedals to rotate. It took many, many years to develop that movement. She did all the therapy programs available to help her achieve. Therapeutic horseback riding was one of her favorite lessons.

I've read that low muscle tone could lead to mild scoliosis, which Jennifer developed in high school. I took her to a specialist, but at her age there was nothing they could do. What I did for her a couple years ago was take her for physical therapy, and they developed a home plan for her. She still does her exercises to this day. Sometimes she gets a massage, which makes her feel good all over, but it mostly helps her back.

Jennifer's balance was always an issue. With time and all her therapies and activities, she is much better, but usually when we are out in the community I put my arm out for her to grab while we walk. Escalators are difficult for her to maneuver. She also does not have the best rhythm. I read that CHARGE children who have hearing loss due to malformations of the inner ear also have problems with balance because the vestibular system is malformed. I don't know if this is why Jennifer has a balance problem.

Survival rate is 70% up to five years old. The first year of life has the highest death rate. I can say that Jennifer's toughest year was her first. She had so many severe problems. When she was born, she had so many complications. The breathing difficulties were the worst, but the combination of all her issues (the choanae atresia, the failure to thrive probably due to her chronic illnesses of congenital heart disease and respiratory disorders) made her first year extremely difficult.

When Jennifer didn't start growing, the doctors believed it was because of failure to thrive. She was born three weeks early, which isn't considered premature. She was five pounds and eighteen inches long, which I was told was fairly normal for being three weeks early. She gained weight very, very slowly and barely grew. Those first years I charted her growth and I figured out with her rate of growth how tall she would eventually be.

I calculated Jennifer's height would be 4'9" and that is exactly what her height is today. It is way below the third percentile for an average height. She always looked so pixie-like, so cute and petite. I had hoped she would have grown a little more. She has always looked so much younger than her age.

Dad, Mom, Jennifer, Matthew, and Christopher.

It hurts me that people never gave her credit for her abilities and judged her on her appearance in school and in her trying to get a job now that she is out of college. The frustration of her trying so hard to get work since college and being unsuccessful is tremendous, not just for Jennifer but for her dad and myself as well. All I can think is that this is the way God wants it to be for now, but we will not give up trying. We have to wait for the right time and the right job.

Jennifer's puberty was delayed, which is something that occurs in more than 70% of children with CHARGE. We sought out an endocrinologist during elementary school based on the advice of a therapist who read somewhere about CHARGE and of needing an endocrinology evaluation. Jennifer does have hypothyroid (low thyroid function) and takes medication, but her height did not really increase much with it. Now babies are tested for thyroid levels at birth, as incorrect levels can lead to mental impairment and short stature. Jennifer is also on hormone therapy, but because of her pulmonary hypertension she cannot have a high dose.

The doctor was wrong about her brain; it did grow and she did not have microcephaly. Jennifer does have a mild mental impairment, but it could have been so much worse. She is highly motivated, bright, creative, funny, and always tries her best. She learned to talk (a neurologist said she wouldn't), read, comprehend, ride a bike, and downhill ski, to name a few of her accomplishments in spite of her problems.

Chapter Six

"That was never an option" was Larry's response when this question was put to him:

"Why didn't you feel like running away and throwing in the towel while raising Jennifer?"

It's all in your attitude, so have a positive one.

<u>This chapter is from his perspective of our Jennifer.</u>

She was our child and we felt about her just like our other two children. She was a part of our family, we loved her, and we would do anything to take care of our children and keep them safe. She was always a joy for us, such a pleasure. Even in the midst of all the stressful situations she would smile, her big blue eyes would sparkle, and she would melt our hearts.

I was there for Jennifer's birth and I was nervous. When she was born, she was purple and they got busy working on her while Carolyn was asking if she had all her fingers and toes. I said she did, but knew there was something wrong and didn't tell her. I called Carolyn's mom and dad after pacing around trying to get some answers, but I kept it low key and just told them we had a baby girl. I called my parents, and my mom could tell something was wrong. I just told her the baby was having some trouble but I needed to get back to my wife. A little nurse ran in and got me out of the room and asked me if I wanted to have the baby baptized since the baby was in distress. I could only think of Carolyn and what was I going to tell her. They wanted a name for the baby, and I said Jennifer H. Siewicki. The priest said her middle name just couldn't be an initial, so I said Henrietta so I could get Carolyn's dad's name in there.

The doctor had Jennifer in his arms while she was being baptized. They told me to leave and I looked back. There was a glow in the room, and I knew she was going to be okay. They told me a team was on their way from Children's Hospital of Detroit and I felt better. I knew Jennifer was here for a reason, for bigger things. The doctor tried to put the IV in her head but couldn't. Jennifer was in a lot of pain and I was very sad for her to have to go through that. I had nothing but love for her. When the team from Children's Hospital arrived, they stabilized her and she looked pretty good. As the medical team was bagging her to help her breathe, Jennifer was brought to Carolyn's room. The doctors said they would be busy with Jennifer, so I stayed with Carolyn and went to see Jennifer the next day.

She was just a sweetie. Every time I touched Jennifer, her heart rate would change. She knew her daddy. I always talked to her.

I knew she would survive. She was a special girl. She was

here for a purpose and as far as what the doctors said about her prognosis, I knew she had problems but never believed she wouldn't make it. As far as her being a chore, I never thought that. She was a joy to have. So many times the doctors told us things I just didn't believe. When a doctor said she wouldn't talk, I knew she would. When she did start talking, it was all in sentences and not just one word at a time. That's why I knew she would be better off than the doctors said she would be. I always remembered her big eyes. She was always excited to see me.

I had a customer who had a sick baby and I knew what he was going through. He was lacking funds, so I tried to help him out with his car repair. It turned out he couldn't handle it and left his wife and child. I could not understand that, but I never wanted to judge.

I always told Carolyn that Jennifer was here for bigger and better things. No one fights as hard as she did. If she could fight that hard, then I could fight just as hard for her. I never thought it was too hard that I couldn't do it anymore or it was too much. Even though I was at work, I still had my emotions and feelings. I was always there for Jennifer. I was scared for her. When we went to New York, I was scared. That first day of triple parking, trying to get into a rooming house, I felt we were back in the 1920s. We didn't have a lot of money, so we borrowed from Carolyn's parents and used their car to drive to New York. I felt touched and love from them.

At the hospital, they did a lot of testing and I was scared for Jennifer. She would look up with her big eyes for support. She did so well. She was remarkable. She always advanced and suc-ceeded in her health and accomplishments. I always felt joy for

Jennifer loves her grandma.

Jennifer, just like I felt for my other children. She was the one doing all the work, not us. I know it's been tough even up to today. In high school it was tough. I didn't want to tell Jennifer, but I was sad for her. It would have made things worse.

I always felt she was an angel. I have seen miracles. I never wanted to give up on her because she never wanted to give up. I wished things would be easier for us, but I would never give up. I always said I wanted to give my boys morals, values, and integrity. If I gave them those, they would be good people. I respected my mom and dad for giving me those ideals. I turned out to be a good person.

People say I'm a workaholic, but I don't think I am. I work hard for my family. I want to take care of them, provide for them, and keep them safe. When she went to Oakland University, I knew we had to do anything we had to for her to go. I knew I'd make it work. That's how I am.

I never thought that Jennifer was too much. She was such a fighter, such a joy. She always showed love. She never showed anybody any bitterness. She never gave us any trouble, even through her teenage years. She was daddy's little girl. I always gave all my children 100 percent. I always gave my boys and Jennifer quality time, not quantity. They remember the quality, the fishing, camping, and boating.

Give your child the same opportunities as their siblings.

Chapter Seven

Jennifer's first day of kindergarten.

Jennifer was in a self-contained special education classroom setting from kindergarten through third grade. The whole four years were pretty great for Jennifer. She made friends, played, learned to be a student. The only problem was that the program needed, in my opinion, more academics. But she was happy with school and so was I, other than the lack of academics. The staff was kind and cared about the students. Jennifer became involved in Brownies at school. We weren't part of the school Brownies, but we had our own meetings among our girls in the Special Education Program. That was okay with me because Jennifer had a rough beginning of life and the smaller class size was, at that time, good for her. Too much stimulation would stress her out, so this program was just right. She went to many birthday parties and had all the students to hers as well. She actually was smitten with one of the little boys. I think it was because she was more comfortable with boys because of having two brothers.

Jennifer's Perspective: Elementary School

Jennifer remembers playing with the puppets, which I think is interesting because she is now a member of the Detroit Puppeteers Guild. She still loves puppets. She knows everything there is to know about Jim Henson and even did a parody film/song about him. She remembers some of her old friends' names and some of the fun things they did together. Jennifer remembers being a Brownie doing crafts and earning patches. She remembers some of her teachers. She said her mind is kind of fuzzy. "I do remember my stuffed toy, Georgette, being lost and we made signs about a lost dog and hung it on the bus." She did remember going to catechism at our neighborhood parish and receiving her First Communion. She said she didn't like it. At that time, God was too abstract for her.

Jennifer was diagnosed with pulmonary hypertension while in kindergarten, and the teacher was truly concerned and compassionate about Jennifer's well-being. That was the summer she was enrolled in her first swimming lessons. She loved the water and did a really great job following directions and learning. That was just the beginning of her many, many different types of lessons. We had a four-foot-deep pool in our backyard and Jennifer was able to practice her swimming abilities daily every summer for years. When we went camping in the years to follow, she enjoyed swimming off the boat in the lakes.

Jennifer's Perspective: Her Brothers

I feel that they really love me and I love them even though they pick on me a little bit. They're always so nice to me. They take me out. When we were growing up, they bothered me sometimes. They put me on the shelf. They put me in a closet. They always played with me. They always read stories to me. They always hated when I would play my Mickey Mouse at night. It would wake them up. *(Jennifer would turn it up full blast so she could hear it because she didn't have her hearing aid in at night.)* Hey, I had to get to sleep somehow. *(Giggle.)* My favorite things to do with my brothers were going swimming and going on vacations with them. They helped me with my video games, played Pretty, Pretty Princess with me, played dogs and dead horse with me. They read to me, but I call them "made-up stories" because they were more like made-up stories. I always loved that instead of the usual, "Once upon a time there was a little girl, yada, yada, yada." It was more fun.

While in this school, she went to the activities the school offered to all students: ice cream socials, parent-teacher conferences, and specials. At one point, it seemed that math might be a strong subject for Jennifer, and she was allowed to try taking the math class in the general education program. But

Jennifer with her brothers.

as it turned out, math was not her strong subject. At least she was given the opportunity to try. Jennifer had a school psychologist do some testing on her in either kindergarten or first grade. The psychologist said Jennifer almost had her fooled because she knew the sight word "banana." Apparently she didn't believe in Jennifer, but luckily we did. We gave our daughter a lot of credit even at that young age because we knew what she was made of. If she knew the words she was tested on, why in the world wouldn't she be given credit for knowing them? The psychologist said, "Don't try to teach her anything, it won't increase her IQ." Are you kidding me? She has been taught plenty and continues to learn.

When Jennifer was six years old, just out of first grade, I could tell that there wasn't a curriculum developed toward academics. Jennifer wasn't being taught how to read. That summer, I took Jennifer to a tutor to help her learn to read. By the end of the summer, she was beginning to read with phonics. The method of "Whole Language" wasn't the way to go for Jennifer. The tutor gave me some books she was using to teach Jennifer so she could take them to school for second grade. The program didn't embrace my enthusiasm. By the next summer, I purchased Hooked on Phonics and began teaching her to read myself.

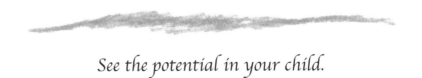

See the potential in your child.

Jennifer was excited to learn, so my part was easy. I remember it was hot and we didn't have air conditioning, but we plugged along trying to get an early start during the cooler part of the day. We worked on it every day, a couple sessions a day. Little by little she was catching on, and by the end of the summer she was a reader. Larry and I always felt that if she could read, the world would open up to her. It was very, very important for her to be able to read. And now look at her, she writes stories and parodies. She even took a creative writing class in college. We are very proud of her.

When Jennifer was in third grade and we were contemplating her next steps (this particular program only went through third grade), I happened to see a segment on the television show *20/20* about a girl who was blind and in a regular classroom setting. A light went on for me, and it was then that I decided that if a blind student could do it, so could Jennifer. I wanted Jennifer to be in our home school, being taught from a curriculum without all the negative behaviors that went along with the self-contained classrooms. I knew that it was Jennifer's right and within the law to learn in the least restrictive environment in school. I went to the Special Education Department and spoke with the Special Education Coordinator and told her we were done with special education. I was going to put Jennifer in our home school in a general education class. She informed me Jennifer didn't have to "quit" special education, that she was entitled to those services that were offered. Jennifer could go to her home school and the services could help her in that school. So that was what we did. We had a new IEP with new goals for Jennifer. I decided to put Jennifer back two grades because of what I considered a loss of instruction and figured this would give her a chance to catch up the best she could. At least she would be exposed to what she had missed up to that point in her education. It was in the IEP that Jennifer was to receive occupational therapy, physical therapy, speech, and services from a hearing consultant. These services would continue through most of her school years.

I'm sure it was difficult for the teachers to initially be prepared for Jennifer (she was one of the first inclusion students), but it was the law and they had to do it. I'm not saying all the teachers did a good job or were accepting, but she was a student there and that was it.

Jennifer blossomed during her elementary school years at her home school. She continued to blossom not only in the school setting but also in the community. She took acting, horseback riding, ice skating, piano, and karate lessons. She also played baseball. Jennifer would go faithfully every week to her different activities (usually more than just one activity) and was always excited to be there.

Jennifer horseback riding.

Jennifer's Perspective: Toys

My favorite toys were Disney toys like a big old talking Mickey Mouse and Goofy. I used to have Sesame Street toys like a big old Big Bird talking toy. I had Bert and Ernie. I had stuffed animals like "Old Brown Doggie" which was actually my brother's, but he let me play with it too. I loved my Roger Rabbit toy I got for Easter one year. I loved my books. I loved books on tape for my talking Mickey Mouse, Goofy, and Big Bird. I loved Goose Bumps books. Even now I like Stephen King, Jeff Dunham, and learning about Howdy Doody books. I love suspense, horror, gore, urban legend, and paranormal books.

Jennifer ran out of breath easily because of her pulmonary hypertension, so we got her an electric scooter to navigate around the school. Most of Jennifer's teachers loved her and did a great job of truly including her in the class. She was happy and made friends (one is still her friend to this day).

In her new elementary school, she participated again in Brownies, field trips, went to more parties, went to School Age Child Care program (an after school program), and school activities like the talent show. There were a few glitches, though. The special education program that was in her school used a playground located at one end of the school, and the general education students used a playground located at the other end of the school. Someone decided Jennifer should use the playground that the special education program used while on recess. A therapist who serviced Jennifer at the school found out and changed that immediately. Jennifer was to be with the students she was going to school with and not be segregated.

The bus Jennifer would take was a shorter bus for special education students. After a while Jennifer wanted to take the typical "big" bus with her neighborhood friends, but the bus stop was on the main street so that wouldn't work for us. One year the "big" bus stop was right in front of our house so Jennifer was able to ride on it. That made her really happy.

Jennifer's Perspective: Elementary School

"Cooper was a good place. I remember show and tell. I remember bringing in some of my stuffed animals." Jennifer mentioned she visited her old sixth grade teacher a couple of years ago. He's now a principal at another school. "I took the small bus, but I really wanted to take the big bus. I did take the big bus one year. I remember doing a Lamb Chop skit at the talent show. It was so cool! I did it with a boy with blond hair. I don't remember his name. I remember playing the game Hi-Ho-Cherry-O. I met my friend Matt B. in fifth or sixth grade."

While Jennifer was in third grade, I finally decided to sign her up for the Make-A-Wish program. Make-A-Wish grants wishes to sick children. At that time, to be considered for Make-A-Wish,

Jennifer being slimed at Nickelodeon Studios, Florida, during the Make-A-Wish trip.

the child had to have a fatal disease. Now the stipulation is a life-threatening disease. It is very difficult to admit to yourself that your child has a fatal disease. Our sons were in high school and I knew they would move on with their lives in the near future, so we needed this family trip to happen soon. Jennifer's wish was to be "slimed" at the Nickelodeon Studios in Florida. We didn't fly because of Jennifer's pulmonary hypertension. She would have to use oxygen on the plane because of the altitude changes and the pressures it could have on her lungs, so we decided to drive. Make-A-Wish set us up for a week-long vacation with a new van to use, a tour of Nickelodeon Studios, and a visit to Disney World. Jennifer had her wish of getting "slimed" as she sat in a little pool at Nickelodeon. It was great. We also had a chance to spend a day at the ocean. We were very grateful that we had this memorable trip with our family.

Jennifer's Perspective: Make-A-Wish Trip

I loved the Make-A-Wish trip! The whole family went. They gave us a van to use. I remember Matthew and Christopher slept the whole way. Christopher had his messy side and Matthew had his clean side. Man, just like now! Some things never change. That's the old saying: Some things never change. He's actually not like that now, but when he was a teenager, his room was something. I got slimed at Nickelodeon Studios. It was so cool. I sat in a little pool and got slimed. I went ahhhhh. I loved it. It was colored applesauce. It was so cool. I should have gotten a job there. If I would have known... Darn it, I should have invented a time machine. I loved going to Disney World because I loved to see all the Disney characters.

My son Christopher, at the time, thought everything was going to be okay with Jennifer. But after going on the Make-A-Wish trip, he thought that maybe she wasn't going to be okay, that maybe she really would die. He said that the Make-A-Wish trip really made him realize the reality of Jennifer's situation.

One school year, Jennifer's resource room teacher became a regular classroom teacher and we felt lucky Jennifer was in her classroom until one of Jennifer's therapists called me at home and told me Jennifer was allowed to "play" in the back of the room with toys while the other students were learning their lessons. When I went to the principal about this matter, she defended her teacher, telling me that she spoke to the teacher, who said it hadn't happened. That teacher made a big turnaround from being a resource teacher to a classroom teacher and it was clear how she felt about a special education student being included in a general classroom. She would give Jennifer really hard tests (not adjusted tests). Jennifer would study and study and would usually pass. But of course the teacher wouldn't give her positive acknowledgment for her grade, stating that she had to study so much more than the other students. Finally, through the new resource teacher, I had the teacher give us a study guide, and that helped. That is what is supposed to happen when a student is struggling; you figure out what needs to be done to make them successful.

Most of Jennifer's other teachers were great. When it was conference time, her sixth grade teacher said he would love to have more time in the classroom with Jennifer and have her go to the resource room less often. Looking back, that's what I should have done, especially since he was an "accepting" teacher. Not all teachers were like him. Jennifer did not have a behavior problem; in fact, she was a riot. She was always friendly, sweet, kind, funny, and hardworking.

I had heard from a mom when Jennifer was in middle school that the department head who arranged for Jennifer to be included in general education was spreading the word that Jennifer was a "model student" for inclusion. I knew she was, but it was nice to hear something positive from school. After another IEP with Jennifer's educational goals determined, I and the school officials thought it would be in Jennifer's best interest to have a one-on-one paraprofessional assist Jennifer in her school day to help her be successful.

Again, this was all pretty new to the school officials, and Jennifer coming to middle school was another experience. The summer before middle school, Jennifer had major surgery on her face for her paralysis. It was pretty rough on her physically, but she made it to school on time, fresh scars and all.

I felt like things were going fairly well at school, and there were no major problems until I was called in for a meeting. I walked into a room with a huge round table full of staff members to basically complain about Jennifer. There was a staff member who actually had a baggie with a broken pencil in it that Jennifer had broken out of frustration. I don't remember if I actually said it, but I thought that if I had a pencil right then I would be breaking it, too. Like mother, like daughter, I guess. They were frustrated because they didn't know how to include Jennifer and it took some work on their part. If I had that meeting to do over, I would put the question to them, "What can the school do to make this work?"

The next year we moved to a new home in the same school district. After researching the various districts that might be the most accommodating, we decided to remain in the same district. What we learned was that the school is only as good as the staff it employs. Jennifer's eighth grade was in a school near our new home. That particular school was wonderful. The school district agreed to my request to begin the new school year bussing Jennifer to the new school from our old house until November when we moved. I really did appreciate that accommodation. Remember, it never hurts to ask. All they can say is no.

We were always nervous at parent-teacher conferences, afraid to get battered. Quite to our surprise, that did not happen at her new school. They seemed to accept Jennifer and focused on her strengths, and they made accommodations where needed. Again she made friendships, went to parties, and attended some after-school activities. Jennifer also had a one-on-one paraprofessional to help her adjust.

I'd have to say the only uncomfortable meeting we had at that school was when Jennifer was at the IEP meeting when she was moving up to the high school. I should have known we were in for trouble when the special education representative from high school was very late, saying she "forgot" about the meeting. Then when we were deciding if Jennifer should be in the special education classes, we mentioned that we didn't know the school even had special education classes. Her response was, "It's the school's best-kept secret."

A comment the paraprofessional made at the meeting was uncomfortable to us when she explained her duties and said that she left Jennifer to take notes on her own and when she came back, Jennifer had hardly written anything down. Apparently she thought Jennifer should have gotten more done even though she knew that was Jennifer's weakness and needed accommodations with that task. Her job was to help Jennifer.

If there was something Jennifer had difficulty with, it was the parapro's job to find a way to make it work. Obviously that was not what she thought. I have seen that same paraprofessional at in-services the school system provides to educate the paraprofessionals, and one of those meetings was about that very subject: how to make the special education student successful, what adaptations need to be made, and what needs to be done to make these things happen. Those questions are golden!

Jennifer finished middle school. She never had a formal tour of the high school with the other students. I didn't know it was offered. I took Jennifer myself during the summer before school started and met with staff and toured the school.

High school was a tough time for us. I hope our struggles during the high school years can somehow benefit other parents. We had another saying on our refrigerator: "high goals, high expectations, high achievement." Those were the words that got us through all of Jennifer's school years, especially high school and after.

Jennifer's Perspective: High School

"Bad memories, bad memories," was Jennifer's reply when asked about her high school days. When asked which classes she enjoyed, Jennifer responded with "The Science and Art and Design Class. I liked my craft class. It was fun. I loved the cooking because after you cooked, you got to eat some samples. I do remember making 'no bake' cookies. We made some *good* cookies. I met some good friends in high school. I was invited to my friend's gymnastic meets. I would have wanted to do gymnastics but, you know, my health and all. Okay, could we skip high school because it was kind of a bad time? There's nothing more for me to talk about, so this interview is over."

A typical experience during the high school years was a conversation I had with Jennifer's cooking teacher, who called me, suggesting her class wasn't appropriate for my daughter. I asked, "What's more important than knowing a little about getting around the kitchen? It's not rocket science." Jennifer even had a one-on-one paraprofessional at her side, so it wasn't like the teacher was being put out in any way or that Jennifer took away from the other students' learning. The teacher simply felt Jennifer should be in a different program. Little did she know what a strong family she was talking to. We didn't go through all that we had endured over Jennifer's school career to be bullied by this teacher. Jennifer continued, did a lot in the class, and seemed to enjoy it. Jennifer must have won the teacher over because an irate teacher can make a student's life miserable, but Jennifer was happy in that class.

A parent can usually kind of get a "feeling" of how things are going in a

Jennifer cooking chili with Uncle Jim.

classroom. I had that "feeling" in Jennifer's math class. Things just didn't feel right, and Jennifer hated her class. I thought it was because she always struggled with math, but I was wrong. The teacher gave her so much grief during class that Jennifer began hiding her unfinished daily assignments from the teacher. It came to light when progress reports came out. Jennifer, never in all her years, reacted to school like that before. It was pretty traumatic for her. I contacted the head of the department, explained the situation, and fortunately it was resolved. Larry and I feel that negative experience has haunted Jennifer's learning about math to this day. She is bright but just cannot get through simple math. It's as if she has a mental block.

But in the community there are ways to adapt for this weakness. Jennifer can use the dollar-more method of paying when the purchase is minor. The dollar-more method is giving singles of the amount of the purchase and handing the cashier an extra dollar for the remaining change. She can also use a calculator when needed. Another strategy she uses is as simple as using a debit card, but you have to make sure there is enough money in the account to cover the purchases. To make her more independent, I have signed her up with online banking that will alert her with an email about her account balance.

When a staff person from the Special Education Department told me not to bother taking Jennifer to Sylvan Learning Center for tutoring because it wouldn't help, it just didn't make any sense to us. Sometimes you have to go with your own common sense and gut feeling about things. Not only did it help Jennifer with her learning, but it gave her confidence and pride.

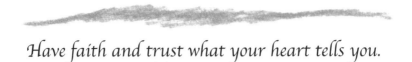

Have faith and trust what your heart tells you.

Our IEP meetings were brutal, but I learned by high school that I needed professionals with me to advocate for Jennifer's best interests. I asked an agency called The Arc (their job is to assist people with challenges to get the most out of their lives) to send a representative to assist at the meetings. I also requested Jennifer's personal agent from the Department of Mental Health to advocate for Jennifer as well. It helps to have professional people at these meetings other than just the parents. Of course this meant having pre-meetings with these representatives so everyone was on the same page.

The mission of an agency we chose from the Department of Mental Health is to provide resources for promoting independence and inclusion of people with developmental disabilities. We have yearly Person-Centered Planning meetings to set goals and ideas about how to achieve those goals, and we also have a budget from the state to assist with Jennifer's various needs. Even though a person can receive services before the age of eighteen, we did not get involved with the Department of Mental Health until Jennifer was eighteen years old.

During Jennifer's last year in high school, she was tested by a school psychologist, and the report described Jennifer nothing like her at all. It contained out-and-out lies about Jennifer. That's the type of treatment our family went through in high school. I didn't want that document in Jennifer's permanent record, so I went to the head of the Special Education Department and had another meeting. It was agreed the school would pay for a private evaluation with a psychologist of my choice. Our psychologist did a thorough, accurate evaluation of Jennifer's strengths and weaknesses, which was submitted to the Special Education Department to be put into Jennifer's file, and the inaccurate evaluation was thrown out.

One of the mistakes I made during these years was that I should have gone to the principal of the school with my concerns. I guess I thought that Jennifer was more of a student of the Special Education Department than of the school as a whole. I only dealt with that department. It would have been one more avenue I could have explored to make Jennifer's high school days more tolerable.

Jennifer continued with her extracurricular activities throughout high school even with the demanding schedule of her homework. When she signed up for an after-school writing club, you'd have thought we'd committed a sin. Her special education staff person was appalled that she signed up without running it by her first. Jennifer did just fine and got a feel for after-school activities. Jennifer was interested in giving the morning announcements at the high school. I asked her special education teacher about this. Then I called the teacher in charge of the announcements. When I didn't get a response back, I went to the school after hours and sought out the teacher asking her to give Jennifer a chance. She said she would look into it, but I never did hear from her. I explained to her that I would practice a script with Jennifer. I knew she could do it, but obviously the teacher had her own thoughts. That setback didn't slow Jennifer down one bit from continuing to gain new experiences on her own.

Encourage your child by providing them with experiences that will help them reach their potential.

It was about that time that Jennifer stopped taking piano lessons after four years so she could pursue violin lessons for a year. This included practicing almost daily as well. She continued her ice skating lessons in 2003 every week all year-round for almost five years until she went away to college in 2008. During these high school years she also played a couple seasons of soccer in Canton, Michigan, for the Rockets, which

Jennifer, the high school graduate.

she loved, and she had more horseback riding lessons, loved it even more, was tutored at Sylvan Learning Center, and sang in the high school chorus. We looked into Jennifer participating in Special Olympics, a sports organization for children and adults with disabilities, but after observing a baseball practice, decided it wasn't for her. The male players on the team were as big as men and Jennifer just stood 4'9". With her medical condition and size, it wasn't suitable for her.

Getting her diploma from high school was HUGE! It entailed lots of hard work on Jennifer's end, as well as ours.

Chapter Eight

After graduating high school in 2004, Jennifer immediately worked part-time at Sylvan Learning Center. She loved her job there. She would restock training materials for the instructors, stamp envelopes, prepare mailings, clean computers and tables, restock and clean the student store, clean up the reception area, and water plants. This was her first experience at using public transportation to get to and from work. In our community, we have special buses that will provide transportation door-to-door. Jennifer's work ethic really shone. She was dependable, never took time off, was never late, and took pride in her work. I'm sure the staff would agree she was a wonderful employee.

Jennifer's Perspective: Sylvan Learning Center

My first job was working at Sylvan Learning Center. I got the job right out of high school. I used to be a student there and they would help with math. I worked there for four years. I quit when I went off to college. I used to stack binders. I set up the school store. I did envelopes, dusted, watered the plants, and cleaned the windows, made sure the tables were

> clean, and got things ready for the kids. I straightened out the magazines in the waiting room. I had a lot of fun there. Made sure everything was in tip-top shape. I would bring a drink and clock in. It was a small clock. You'd have it on the table and press it. I'd say IN. I would get my pop ready in my little office. My iPod, I would get in my ear. I would do some work and I would get a little break in my little office. I loved it. The people were nice. When I quit, they had a pizza party for me. They had cake and presents for me, too.

The next year, Jennifer noticed a door in the building with a Make-A-Wish sign on it. As a former Wish kid, she walked in and asked if she could volunteer after work once a week. That was the beginning of her many, many volunteering positions. While she was volunteering in that office, she saw a 4'x5' poster hanging on the wall of a shiny new red Corvette being raffled off at the Woodward Dream Cruise that summer. She had just received her driver's permit, so her grandma bought Jennifer a raffle ticket–and it was THE WINNING TICKET. Grandma's luck was passed on to her granddaughter. Oh, how exciting! There is never a dull moment in our household.

Jennifer's Perspective: Winning the Corvette

I had a strong feeling I could win. This was a contest for me. Of all the other contests I ever entered that I did not win, this was a contest for me because I knew I was going to win the car and this was a contest for me.

Grandma, Mom, Dad, and Jennifer with the winning Corvette.

It was a 6-speed and Jennifer really wanted to drive it, so we took her to a very large parking lot and with her dad next to her and me with my camera, I was able to take a picture of my beautiful daughter actually driving the Corvette. She never made it out of first gear but nevertheless, she did drive it.

Jennifer kept busy in the community with activities that included volunteering with the Livonia Jaycees, the Michigan Humane Society, Make-A-Wish Foundation of Michigan, and Project Linus (making blankets for the local children's hospital). She joined Michigan Adaptive Sports and learned to downhill ski beginning from sitting in a chair to now standing. She also learned to water ski and kayak. She joined Programs to Educate All Cyclists (PEAC) to learn to ride a two-wheeler bike and enjoys family rides with the group on Thursday evenings.

Downhill skiing with Michigan Adaptive Sports.

She became a member of the Detroit Puppeteers Guild and attends their events, even those out-of-state. Jennifer loves puppeteering and learned much about her idol, Jim Henson. She took private ice skating lessons and even though her lips would turn blue because she would run out of breath and didn't have the best balance so it was a lot harder to skate, she took lessons every week for several years.

With her love for animals, Jennifer still enjoys horseback riding. Her therapeutic riding facility closed, so we went to a local regular riding stable for a few years but were refused riding lessons the fourth year, stating they didn't think she could handle the riding. I know, it didn't make any sense to me either and I did file a formal complaint with the state, but we did move on to private lessons from an occupational therapy instructor for another few years until they closed. Now Jennifer rides with the Oakland County 4-H Proud Equestrian Program at the Bloomfield Open Hunt Club and is happy once again.

Jennifer's Perspective: Animals

I love all animals big or small, wild or tame. Animals are part of the world, part of our life. We wouldn't be here without them. If we don't take care of the animals, life would cease to exist. Like the anteaters reduce the bug population and the bees do the honey. It's all part of nature. I love taking care of animals. I wanted to be a vet doctor but that was one thing you said I couldn't do because of the math.

After the dust settled that fall, Jennifer enrolled in a Media Production class at Madonna University. Jennifer was always interested in media and Madonna University offered TV courses. I went to the Office of Disabilities and made my pitch for Jennifer to audit the classes. The instructor was contacted and was onboard with it. Jennifer was ready to audit the class. We would drop her off at school in the evening. Through a window in the building, we could see her climb the stairs to the second floor while we sat in the parking lot. I was more nervous than she was, I'm sure. My heart raced but slowed down a little bit each week she went. Here was my special education student with huge medical issues to deal with and a cognitive impairment, but she finished the class and did a fantastic job.

Jennifer's Perspective: Madonna University

Madonna was really great. I really liked making movies like "Jason." I did it with my brothers. I was Jason of course. And I liked making that music video, "Ghostbusters." Working the cameras was kind of hard for me because it cricked my neck, so the instructor put a box or something I could stand up on, but I really liked working with the editing part. But I really liked being right there, front and center, being the star of the film I made. Too bad I didn't use fake blood in one of my movies. We could have just used ketchup. But it was really good. I loved it. I felt a little nervous when I first started taking classes, but I got used to it. I miss those days.

Jennifer in the Madonna University Video Production class.

Jennifer did so well that she enrolled in the Video Editing class at Madonna in September 2006. Again, she worked really hard and did just fine. She produced and edited a couple of movies, with her brothers as actors, and had a really enjoyable time doing it. The school's policy was that a student could audit only two classes, so Jennifer was done.

The instructor told me the classmates, Jennifer included, were joking around with each other and another instructor overheard them and was concerned they were joking unkindly about Jennifer, but her instructor told her that that's not how it was at all. They truly enjoyed Jennifer and she enjoyed them. I was told by the Office of Disabilities after Jennifer's Madonna experience that because of Jennifer they were considering a program for the students at a local Special Education School to be part of Madonna. Already Jennifer is a positive influence in the community.

In 2007, Jennifer continued working at Sylvan Learning Center and enjoyed her other activities, such as ice skating and being a member of a local civic group for young people, the Livonia Jaycees. During this time, she was asked by the Friends of CLS (Community Living Services) if she would be interested in enrolling in an eight-week Television Production Certification Training Program at Community Media Network in Troy, Michigan. The Friends of CLS were aware of Jennifer's passion for the media. Of course, Jennifer jumped at the chance to participate. We drove her across town during rush hour every week for two months to make her dream come a little closer.

When the class was over, Jennifer received an email from the Community Media Network with information about a three-day George Michael's Actor's Workshop in a nearby community. I attended alongside with Jennifer to take notes and together we got more information on acting and what was involved.

That fall, Jennifer enrolled at Schoolcraft College, in Livonia, Michigan, and took an online creative writing class and later an online veterinary assistant class. She has a lot of interests dear to her heart. She took the online veterinary assistant class because she has a closeness with animals that is obvious to everyone around her.

She also loves to write stories and make movies. She has some of her work posted on YouTube. She even submitted one of her stories to a Hollywood producer but it was returned along with a letter stating, "In the future, have your people contact our people." I asked Jennifer who her people were and we agreed it was just me, and we laughed and laughed. At least she makes attempts at her dream of working in Hollywood. She still thinks outside the box and gets creative with her ideas of contacting producers. Currently she has been exchanging emails with a producer. You can't tell where it might lead.

Jennifer's Perspective: What Do You Love to Do?

I love to write stories. Watch Animal Planet, Nat-Geo-Wild. I love to play with my dog, Cindy, and take care of her because of her bad back. I love her to death. So much. Eat, I like to go out to eat sometimes, go to the movies. I love to horseback ride. It's good to get out of the house and do something. It's fun. I love riding horses and taking care of them after I ride. I put the saddle on them, I love brushing them, feeding them an apple, brushing their tails, getting them all ready, cleaning their hoofs. I like to be busy, busy, busy even though my parents are, and that's okay, darn it I can't say the o-l-d *(spelled it)* word, ahh getting less active, yeah, how about that, that's a better way to say it. *(We take her to most of her activities.)*

I love the paranormal. I tried to join a paranormal activities club at Oakland University, but it was so hard for me because I didn't have transportation to get to the locations and it was pretty late at night. They go to different events and try to talk to ghosts. And I love that stuff. I even watch it on the Travel Channel. I recently went to a psychic and a séance with my sister-in-law, Shera. It was really cool. It was at a haunted house, but it didn't look like it was haunted. I like real haunted houses not the fake ones. It doesn't really scare me; it just excites me. It gives me a tingling feeling. It just gives me the feeling that, **YES**, I think ghosts are real.

Later that year, Jennifer, Larry, and I attended a dinner hosted by The Arc of Northwest Wayne County, Redford, Michigan, where Jennifer was presented with the Georgie Rudin Award for self-determination. We were all so very proud. It was so refreshing to have Jennifer recognized for her accomplishments in spite of her challenges.

At the end of the summer of 2008, after four years of working at her job, Jennifer decided to quit and pursue her dream of going to college and of living on her own.

Chapter Nine

The winter of 2008 was probably the most important turning point in Jennifer's life. She applied, interviewed for, and was accepted into a new OPTIONS Program at Oakland University in Rochester Hills, Michigan. This was a three-year program designed for people with disabilities to attend a university and to get the full experience of campus life. The director of the program saw in Jennifer what we saw: a person full of life, hard-working, dedicated, and with big dreams. We will always be grateful that she was given this amazing opportunity.

An Oakland University student!

Jennifer's Perspective: What Makes You Continue to Learn and Grow as a Person?

Well, I think it's you guys. Because you guys always tell me to go for it. You guys help me with everything. I think all your words and all your love and care really inspire me to do more than I can. And I love you.

Because she wasn't going for a degree and the classes were considered as being audited, she was not eligible for any student loans or grants for the tuition. We were committed to the idea of college and felt this was a chance of a lifetime for our high-spirited daughter with big dreams. This opportunity also meant that Jennifer would have her own apartment during the school year for the next three years. To look at our petite daughter, others were skeptical about this endeavor, but WE KNEW she could do it with assistance. We tried to get Jennifer a roommate, but the apartment we chose, which was most suited for her and in the Rochester area for the bus, was eight miles from school. It was a little farther than the other students wanted to travel. Jennifer's personal agent, Ann Mansour, from CLS of Oakland County, was phenomenal at helping us adjust to the new living arrangements and life at school. She even recommended the best staff to help Jennifer travel back and forth to Livonia on weekends, and help her with shopping, homework, and cleaning her apartment. The Arc was with me every step of the way to help us make this happen. I called them all the time. But the best was when they helped me get a budget to help with staffing and transportation. An Arc representative ALWAYS came to any meeting I requested. They were always there for Jennifer and, in turn, her family.

Jennifer's Perspective: Trying Really Hard When Attempting Something New

I think it's because I always tell myself I think I can, I think I can, all the courage built up inside me. I just say hey, just go for it. **Do you ever think you can't do something? Does** jump-roping count? **Do you ever think it's harder for you than most people?** Sometimes, sometimes, but not too much. I just think I can do it. **Do you see yourself as a person with challenges?** Not really. I just see myself as a person with glasses and a hearing aid, that's it. Just a normal everyday Joe. Joanette. Joanette because I'm a girl. The girl next door.

It wasn't easy setting up Jennifer's new life at college. I was not getting any support from my local Department of Mental Health agency. They actually gave me the most grief about her attending college. It wasn't until I was able to get my Oakland County personal agent, Ann (again with the help and advice from The Arc), to help get things turned around.

That summer before school, Jennifer and I made many trips to Rochester Hills to get things ready for her. We looked and looked for the right apartment complex that could accommodate her electric scooter. We went to the bus yard and personally measured the bus opening to make sure the scooter would fit between the door opening. I spent the first week with Jennifer and accompanied her for the bus ride to school to make sure there were no glitches. We made many trips to the campus, checking out her classrooms and the best route to take. The most important thing for Jennifer to know was that if she got lost, all she had to do was to ask any student for directions. That is what any other student would do.

Jennifer's Perspective: College Apartment

I loved my college apartment. It was big. It was so nice. I had my own entertainment center, my own computer. I had a bedroom, living room, and a kitchen by the living room so I didn't have far to walk. I could make my own food. Well, you sent food, too, but I warmed it up. I love to cook and I loved my apartment. I'm using this couch I had in my living room. I used to sleep on it sometimes when I didn't have school the next day. I wasn't nervous when I lived in my apartment. I was very happy. Only sad part was moving out. The only thing that bugged me was the thermostat. It was always too cold, then it was too hot, try to do it in the middle *(put the dial)* it's like, aww forget it. I couldn't get the temperature right. But, anyway, I did have a fun time.

Jennifer would take a bus to school every day and would maneuver around campus in her electric scooter. By the third year of school, she knew all the shortcuts around campus and was a very confident student. She was always having lunch with other students that were around. She was a very happy young woman.

Jennifer's Perspective: Public Transportation

The bus ride was great. It was kind of bumpy but I liked it like that. The bus came right to my house. I gave the driver my ticket and he punched it. Here they were nice, but at Oakland they were mean to me when I called to change the time or asked to be picked up early. Sometimes I had to call a taxi. I'd just say, "Forget the bus, I'm calling Len. I don't care how much it costs. Hi Len!" We would talk about Chucky and the old days. We would talk about horror movies. I still have his number. I'm going to keep it.

82

Jennifer's major was Communications. She took three or four classes every semester. She took everything from the History of Rock and Roll to Anthropology. She was referred to as a "model" student. She not only did all of her homework but attended her classes faithfully.

Jennifer's Perspective: College vs. High School

They (college) accepted me for who I was. I wasn't like a little fish in a big ol' pond anymore. I wasn't like the weakest of the pack, you know like lions have the weak one and they always pick on the weak one. I was like the strongest. I was like the biggest thing you could ever see. Everybody was different just like me. Some people had challenges. But, I felt **good**. I felt normal. I felt "hey, you know, since high school didn't give me two seconds." High school got me in a bad feeling that nobody liked me. The kids liked me, but some of the teachers... *It's not that they didn't like you; it's just that they didn't think you belonged there.* Right, exactly, but they were wrong. I was supposed to be there. I did belong there. I don't know. I just didn't like high school that much. It wasn't the kids; it was the teachers. Let's just put it this way, I was like a prey animal and there was all these carnivores trying to eat me! The staff, not the kids. In college, the staff and kids accepted me. I loved the staff. They were all very funny, generous, and nice. They helped me. I had some friends that helped me with my homework, Christie and two different Kellies and Nicole. I wish I could go back.

She joined many clubs, from a sorority to trying to join a Paranormal Club but didn't have transportation to the locations. She had her own radio show at WXOU, the campus radio station. She volunteered to help the students at the Oakland University

Cares Film Camp. It's a two-week camp during the summer at Oakland University with Joey Travolta, John Travolta's brother, and a crew from Hollywood, California. The students of the camp are autistic and learn how to put on a film production. Jennifer loved it so much that she still signs up to volunteer each summer, taking a cab from Livonia, or friends or family driving.

Jennifer's Perspective: College Life

I loved college. The campus was great. I loved eating at the cafeteria. I loved buying pizza there. I loved riding my scooter around campus. I loved my professors. I loved all my classes except for the Anthropology class. I didn't really hate it, but it was just so darn hard. I mean, I ain't going to lie. I met some good friends there. I still talk to Nicole. I just talked to her yesterday. We're getting together next week. My best thing was media, learning about radio. I loved working at the radio station. I was a DJ *(sigh)*. Even though I didn't have much to talk about, I still loved to do the music. Sometimes I'd run out of ideas, you know. That's life.

When Jennifer was starting out in college, we heard about a couple of programs we thought would be useful for her. "Dragon Speaks" is a program where one speaks and it types what is said, and "Kurzweil," Jennifer's favorite, a program that can read what is printed. That one was a godsend as she had lots of books to read for school. After some research, emails, and phone calls, we contacted the Ladies of the Lions and they generously donated the programs to Jennifer. We were very grateful.

In 2011, Jennifer received her certificate of completion from Oakland University. What a wonderful three years it had been. It was a lot of work for a lot of people but worth every moment of it. Many times people with challenges aren't given a chance and say "they can't" while we taught Jennifer to say "I can try."

Christopher thought Jennifer's drive to go away to college and live alone in an apartment was amazing. He was so very impressed that she did all of that. Every step for Jennifer was a big deal. Jennifer has a strong personality. It's who she is. But he still worries about her, that she'll find her way.

Since college, Jennifer has been looking for work in the television, film, and radio industry as well as typical, local jobs but without success. We've tried what seems like everything. Jennifer has emailed and mailed some of her works (she writes stories and parodies) to people she looks up to, such as Steven Spielberg and Caroll Spinney. Jennifer would love to work on the documentary about Caroll Spinney. You can watch some of her work on YouTube-Horrorfan 436. She even put in an application to Sesame Street just last week.

Jennifer's Perspective: Applying for a Job and Not Being Hired

I don't know. I think it's because I'm out of college. I'm done. It's like "you have to have a college degree." *(Jennifer received a certificate of completion.)* Sometimes I really think they have other college kids to worry about. But, it's okay. I'll keep trying. That Radio Disney sounds promising and that vet hospital does too. I'm not overly concerned about it. I'm calm. I'm looking into an online radio show. I have a website to check out.

Jennifer has big dreams and I know some day her dreams will come true, but the journey to that dream is a bumpy road. All it will take is one person to give her a break. Everyone deserves a break. Jennifer says, "No one takes me seriously" when applying for a job. She is very talented, creative, dependable, and hardworking and would be an asset to any employer, given the chance. Did I mention she is a riot? I'd be very surprised if she doesn't bring you joy after several minutes of meeting with her.

Jennifer has always been an inspiration to both of her brothers. Matthew comments that it's amazing all that she's accomplished despite the challenges she's overcome. "She has shaped who I am now." Christopher feels that his sister has molded him. "I think I am more affectionate to my own family because of her."

> ### Jennifer's Perspective:
> ### Applying for a Job and Not Giving Up
>
> I think it's my confidence. I think it's because I know I have to get a job, I think I might get a job, I just keep trying, like that little engine that could. Just keep chugging, I think I can, I think I can. It's like *come on people, hire me already!*

Other hopes and dreams of Jennifer are typical of most young people. She wants to have a career, get her own place (preferably a condo), a husband, and more pets. Of course, I am always calling my local Arc affiliate to help facilitate these dreams. Someone from The Arc has attended and facilitated every yearly Person-Centered Plan Jennifer has had throughout the years. It gives us peace of mind knowing an organization is there to be "on our side." The Department of Mental Health is supposed to do things in the best interest of their client, but don't forget they are going to try to hold onto monies from the state the best they can.

Another resource I'd recommend is going to every "After I'm Gone" program The Arc presents. Knowledge is power, and we as parents will not be around for our children forever. We need to make them as independent as they can be and have safeguards set up for them for when we are gone.

Chapter Ten

It's true that some parents could not handle their medically fragile baby/child and would leave or give the child up. We, as parents of such a baby, said we would never judge other parents on how they handled their situations. It was tough—very, very tough. Nobody asks for this for their beautiful new baby. The reality of it is, it happens. I can honestly say we never asked, "Why us, why our baby?" We didn't like it. We would have chosen for our child to be born healthy and not go through long stays in the hospital, many tests, and pain. When she was a year or two old, I would have to shut the windows in the summer because the neighbor's little girls were outside running around and squealing like little girls do, while my little girl was in a bouncer being tube fed, vomiting, and having her tracheotomy suctioned. I felt guilty about Jennifer's problems. Not that I did anything wrong, but my rationale was that because she came out of my body, I was responsible. It took me years not to feel like that. There was never one thing that changed my thinking. I figured it was part of the "grief process." You do grieve for the baby that you thought you were going to have. I didn't know she wasn't going to be healthy.

My husband and I got through our days by supporting each

other, talking through our problems, and doing the best we could to cope. In the beginning, we had 24/7 private-duty nurse care, so we had our moments together. We would wait for "shift change" at 11 p.m. and either go on the porch and enjoy the air or go out for an hour. Our night nurse, Fran, was one of the best. She was very comfortable with Jennifer from day one. She loved our Jennifer. Sometimes I would wake up at night hearing the two of them playing. She would dress Jennifer up in one of her cute little dresses and comb her hair and sing to her.

Jennifer did require a lot of care. Some people might think that I had it covered; the nurses did everything for me. They could not know what it really was like because they did not live through it. And no one takes better care of their child than their mom or dad. Larry had his own auto repair garage and he spent most of his day at the shop making a living to take care of his family. We definitely needed the insurance coverage. I was able to stay home and take care of the children. Some days got so frazzled for me that I would enjoy the chance to take the garbage out to the back of the yard, just to have a couple moments to myself and breathe. Larry said he knew I would take good care of our little baby. I also had a lot of faith in God to help me through those wild days. Heck, I still ask God to give me strength to help Jennifer be the best she can be and to achieve her goals. I always prayed for the doctors to know what to do, too.

My sons loved their sister right from the start. They loved to visit Jennifer in the hospital as a newborn. They fought over who would sit by her. They playfully teased her as she got older and they still do. They would always ask how the baby was doing.

They did cross-patterning with her for five years with never a complaint. (Cross-patterning is a motor skill of having to move her right arm forward along with her left leg, and vice versa to exercise the brain.) They would think it was funny when I asked them to "be with their sister" instead of babysitting her. I told them you couldn't "babysit" your own family member. They played with her, even Pretty, Pretty Princess, putting all the jewelry on including a tiara, which was part of the game. Reading to her in her bed until not only Jennifer but Matthew or Christopher fell asleep. Even having people in our home 24/7 for three years didn't seem to bother them. They went about their business of school and playing like normal. This life was our normal.

One of the hardest things I did for Jennifer (next to signing her up for the Make-A-Wish program) was to see a lawyer about a Special Needs Trust. Doing so gave truth to the matter that Jennifer may have trouble with gainful employment to support herself in the future. When Jennifer was a young teen, and after going to an "After I'm Gone" meeting presented by The Arc of Northwest Wayne County, Larry and I decided it was time to see a lawyer to get all the legal matters in order for our sons and for Jennifer. We went to a lawyer who specialized in drawing up a Special Needs Trust on Jennifer's behalf. A Special Needs Trust is a specialized document to preserve governmental benefits and protect assets. We also had our will refreshed at the same time. The service was expensive, but we felt it had to be done to ensure Jennifer's future.

Another thing we learned from an "After I'm Gone" meeting was about insurances and how the policies could be set up in Jennifer's behalf. We purchased a whole life insurance policy called "Second to Die," which means that after we both pass, Jennifer would receive a cash benefit to her Special Needs Trust.

Chapter Eleven

Over the years, more and more treatments have come out for pulmonary hypertension. No cure has been discovered yet, but we are hopeful. At this point, if Jennifer were to get worse, she would need a heart/lung transplant. Of course we pray that more new medications will be developed.

In 2000, Jennifer was included in a study for UT-15 (now called Remodulin). It is a very powerful liquid drug given with a subcutaneous injection that goes through a line from a pump that Jennifer wears 24/7. Around the same time, other drugs were beginning to be used through a port in the chest, but fortunately Jennifer benefited from the UT-15. That was another very, very scary hospital visit. We didn't know how she would react to the medicine and were fearful because if she's off of it for even a few hours, she gets extremely sick (which happened once when she was at college). If that should happen, she would have to start the medication over again with a low dose and increase it over a few days to a level she could tolerate. When this did happen, I wanted to take her to the ER at the University of Michigan Hospital. They told me I was doing everything they would do and that they wouldn't be able to do anything differently to make her feel better. She just had to work through it.

> ### Jennifer's Perspective:
> ### Her Health and What She's Afraid of
>
> I think my health is okay. I don't worry about it. Okay, I'm going to take my pills and I'm going to be okay and be done. Get up, take a shower, take my pills, and that's it. Get on with it. I never worried except for you guys but that's it. I'm never scared about my health. I never say why me. I'm always so good. I'm not really scared, except of clowns, but that's another story. *(Ha-ha.)*

When she was first put on UT-15, the concern for Jennifer was site pain. Apparently that can be a huge side effect. That is why it was such a big decision to start her on that medication or the one that went in a port. The port medication had its own problems. It had to be on ice and worn in a backpack. It had to be mixed and only had a shelf life of one day. We chose the UT-15. Jennifer was the only patient who **did not** experience site pain. It was another miracle. It helped her shortness of breath, and she is still on it to this day along with a lot of other drugs developed for pulmonary hypertension. We are hopeful technology keeps up with Jennifer as PH is a progressive, life-threatening disease. She is doing amazing!

Jennifer's Perspective: Worry

I worry about my parents. I feel that if I move away, who will take care of you like you take care of Grandma? I worry about you like you worry about me and my brothers. Will I ever get a husband or have a boyfriend? Every time I go to these dances or social events, the guys are just too old or too young or something. I need something in the middle, someone my own age. Like not too hot, not too cold, just right. Like "Hey, do you want to go out for a root beer float, Jennifer?" "**Sure**, let's talk about our families." (*Ha-ha, just kidding.*)

After beginning the new therapy, we went back to New York every three months the first year for check-ups. We were told at that time that she could not be off the meds for more than a half hour, so that meant we could not be farther than one half hour from her. She couldn't go to Grandma's in Irish Hills anymore unless I was with her in case she needed medication or there was a pump problem. If we went any distance, we always took her medical bag with all the things in it for a site change.

As the years went on, it was discovered that a patient could be without the medication for a couple of hours with no serious side effects. Jennifer could go to her grandma's for a few days (the pump syringe needs medication added to it every three days) because even if there were a pump problem, we could be there in one hour and fifteen minutes.

When Jennifer went away to college, she was only forty-five minutes away, and again this was doable. We had a nurse add to the pump during the middle of the week, and when Jennifer was home on the weekends we changed the pump and the site. It hasn't been perfect—she's had a couple of hospital stays for serious infections at the site—but overall, Remodulin has saved Jennifer's life.

Our pet therapy dog, Cindy.

Jennifer's Perspective: Goals/Plans for the Future

My plan is to move out of this house, get a husband, new dogs even though I have Cindy (our pet dog), keep her around. I would like to live in a condo or maybe a little apartment, but a condo would be nice with a pool. I would like to live in Hollywood. I would like to get a job in TV or radio, films, or plays. I write my own stories. It's fun. But the problem is to make up my own characters in the stories. I use someone else's characters. I write songs and parodies. Maybe I should contact Weird Al and send him my parodies and say, "Hey, you write parodies and so do I. Maybe we could hook up? Think about it." Not too long ago I submitted a story, a sequel to *Who Framed Roger Rabbit?* to Robert Zemeckis, the director of *Who Framed Roger Rabbit?*. I got it back with a letter saying, "Have your people call my people." And I'm like seriously, I'm your biggest fan over here. I want to help you. This sequel isn't going to move itself, you know. I also put an application out to Sesame Street in New York City. I love puppeteering. I really love puppets. I loved Sesame Street.

Please see the Appendix for samples of Jennifer's stories.

Jennifer singing a song she wrote at karaoke night.

When Jennifer was diagnosed with CHARGE, we were told that only 200 children had been diagnosed with CHARGE as well. Now the number is 1 in 8,500–10,000. It was two years ago that Larry went on the Internet to see if there was any information on CHARGE because we were trying to get creative with helping Jennifer and her social life. We thought maybe there were other people with CHARGE we could meet up with. It turns out that there is a whole website on CHARGE and they have yearly conferences. I contacted the president of the organization to see if there were any local support groups. She did send me a list of other people with CHARGE in our surrounding area. I haven't contacted anyone yet, but it's on my list of things to do.

Jennifer's Perspective: Her Friends

Matt B. is still a really great friend. I've known him since 5th grade. We've done a lot of fun things together. He likes to tease me. I like to tease him too. He's funny. Then there's Sara. I met her at the bike program *(PEAC)*. She still comes over every week. She helped me with homework in college. Now she's trying to help me get a job. We do a lot of fun stuff together. We go to the mall. We do stories. I love being around my friends. I love being around my parents and my brothers. I love spending time with my nieces and nephews. I wish I could see them even more.

I have never been a big support group person. Jennifer's medical issues always hurt deeply, and I couldn't really share my feelings about it with others. But I am ready now and would actually love to meet other young people like Jennifer. I see some pictures of children on the website and they definitely resemble Jennifer as a child. I think the parents would love to meet Jennifer and see what kind of wonderful person she is. She is a very happy young woman with big dreams who brings so much joy. I think she would be an inspiration to families to see what their child can possibly become in spite of such a medically rough life. The first three years were definitely the hardest. We got through it because we never gave up HOPE.

Jennifer's Perspective: Fear of God as a Child

Now I'm not afraid. I know God loves me and I love God. I pray to Jesus. I pray. I think he's helping me with all these challenges. I think I'm going to get a job. I think God is helping me through life.

I know it can be difficult, but any family facing challenges with their children, whether medical or just typical challenges, needs to BELIEVE, have hope and faith. If both parents are raising the family together, each can depend and lean on the other, just like we did. If not, do not be afraid to reach out to other family members or friends. Helping others gives people joy and meaning. It actually helps to talk, plan, and even cry about the situation.

Jennifer with Grandma, her brothers, sisters-in-law, nieces, and nephews.

Here are some things to remember when raising a medically challenged child:

• Allow yourself to fall apart, to grieve for the way you thought things should have been. An old saying that fits, "Dust yourself off and pick yourself up."

• Try to keep moving forward. Be strong.

• Try to find out as much as you can that pertains to your situation so you have a better handle on things. If you don't know the answers, ask someone who might know.

• Be an advocate for your child.

• Find the right teacher/school so your child can be successful. Remember to ask, "What can the teacher/school do to make this work?"

• It never hurts to ask, so be sure to do so.

• Request a class schedule that will enhance and inspire your child's success.

• Remember to provide community experiences that help your child adapt.

• Seek out agencies to help your child now and for when you won't be able to help.

• Become aware of services such as the Special Needs Trust.

• Keep current on medical changes that can benefit your child.

Chapter Twelve

Our 7,200-mile cross-country road trip.

In July 2012, Larry and I took a five-week cross-country motorcycle ride. This was the vacation of a lifetime. If our sons and their wives did not take over our responsibilities with Jennifer, it would have never happened. They were onboard with the idea right from the beginning. Jennifer was great too. She was very happy for us. She does realize how much we do for her on a daily basis. She's always thanking us. I'll ask her, "Thank you for what?" Her response is simply, "For everything." While we were gone, she took care of the house, herself, and the dog without any problem. When she lost power and the house alarm on the basement ceiling wouldn't shut off, she took it upon herself to go downstairs with a flashlight and bang on the alarm with a broom handle. It still was sounding, but she did what I probably would have done.

We didn't make advance reservations or tell our friends who lived around the country that we were planning to visit. I didn't get excited until the day we left. Our life is so unpredictable that nothing is set in stone. Jennifer could get an infection at her site where the infusion pump catheter is inserted, or she may have an adverse reaction to the specialized medication at any given time.

It took a lot of planning to make this trip, which included lists, lists, and more lists: names of all her doctors and their phone numbers, a list of all her medications, when and where to order them, making sure all refills were up-to-date, a list of all her personal information in case something happened to us. That led to lists of all our personal information for the same reason. We made a list of her friends, agencies, and names we deal with on her behalf, lists of her activities, times, numbers, and locations, a list of appointments she had, and one of the biggest folders was that of her job hunting. That also included her applications, résumés, and where she had already applied.

We contacted her cardiologist and told him what we were thinking of doing and asked for any recommendations he might have. We contacted the Visiting Nurse Association we used when Jennifer was in college. The nurses used to add to

Jennifer's pump during the week while she was in college. My sons and their wives had to be trained on inserting the cannula on Jennifer's 24-hour subcutaneous infusion pump. They came over for a period of two months to practice on Jennifer while we were present. They needed training on adding to the pump every other day, how to fill up the pill boxes, and how to order the pills. I ordered her specialty drugs myself while on vacation from an out-of-town pharmacy. The family split up the task of shopping with and for Jennifer. I left a list of things she might need weekly and they could build from that.

Then it was Jennifer's turn for training and more lists. I had to teach her how to do her own laundry. I made up a template she could follow on how to wash and dry certain clothes. And we practiced and practiced and practiced. There was a list about our dog and when to give her pills, as well as the veterinarian's name and number. I had to teach Jennifer how to clean her bathroom all by herself. Again, there were more papers on that. She already knew how to clean the rest of the house, so that was one less thing. She took care of her dog, Cindy, my plants, the house, made phone calls, visited her grandma, and most importantly, took care of herself as much as she could.

Larry had to get the motorcycle ready. There were a lot of bike accessories needed for the trip. That meant researching each accessory, ordering, and installing them. He literally installed the last item the day we left. In fact, it was getting so late in the day when we were leaving that we almost left a day later, but decided that two hours on the road would be better than none.

We bought an iPad and a camera for Jennifer's computer so we could Skype and send pictures to her email. While we were traveling around this beautiful country of ours, we sent pictures to our friends and family so they could "join us" on our travels. Everyone was so excited for us. People know how much responsibility we have and what a big thing this was for us to do.

Every morning when I got on that bike, I was so excited for the new day. We had headphones if we wanted to listen to music, but we really didn't use them too much because we enjoyed listening to the sounds of the road, of our travels, engrossed in thought and prayer. It was especially peaceful in the early mornings with that little haze over the road. That was the best. I used to say that heaven for me would be lying on a sandy beach soaking up the sun. Now I would have to say it would be one continuous "ride," just like our trip.

People have often told us how "wonderful" we are, but we just couldn't see us doing things any other way for any of our three children. We are very devoted parents, especially when one is hurting and needs help. Everybody is different and handles life's challenges in their own way. When we hear someone "ragging" on parents, we stand up for those parents because some people just can't handle it. It doesn't make them bad parents. They are probably doing the best they know how. I feel very fortunate to have Larry as my children's dad because he is my rock. He always knows what to say to ease my concerns and sometimes we just hold each other until we can regroup. Even in our scariest times, Larry would say to me, "Don't worry; we'll figure out how to make it happen." And you know what… we always do. It might take awhile, but we have faith. It might not work out exactly how we envisioned it would or should, but it does work out one way or another.

If after reading our story you walk away with a few truths,

then Jennifer's purpose in this world is further established.

When I feel backed into a corner, I decide to form a plan that may help me get to my goal. It gives me power instead of hopelessness.

Try not to be too hard on yourselves. The old saying of "we are only human" really fits. This is one I still struggle with but am working on continuously.

Reach out to others and take the help that's offered. It will be a blessing for you and for your family. People need other people. We are in this together.

Stay focused on your child's strengths, their hopes and dreams, and build on that.

I have a saying on my refrigerator: "Entrust your works in the Lord and your plans will succeed." Personally, I don't know how I would have gotten through my struggles without my faith. I always ask for strength and to know what to do. I pray for the doctors to know what to do. I pray for my family. It is difficult to accept bad things, but what we do is ask, "What can we do to make things better?" You always have to give yourself a pep talk. I feel if I at least keep trying, it gives me hope for the better. Never give up. Your children need you. If you don't give it your all, who will?

Appendix

I'm Already There:
A Tribute to Jim Henson's Memory

By horrorfan436
(Jennifer's adaptation of Lonestar's
"I'm Already There," written by Gary Baker,
Frank J. Myers, Richie McDonald, 2001 BMG Entertainment)
Warning: This song may make you cry.

He called him on the phone
from a local hospital
just to hear him say goodbye one more time.
And when he heard the sound
of the Muppets laughing in the background,
he had to wipe away a tear from his eye.
A little Kermit came on the phone
and said Jim when you coming home?

He said the first thing that came to his mind,
I'm already there.

Take a look around.
I'm the sunshine in Ernie's hair.
I'm Bert's paper clips.
I'm the whisper in the wind.
I'm Big Bird's imaginary friend.
And I know I'm in your prayers.
Oh, I'm already there.

He got back on the phone,
said I really miss you, Jim Henson.
Don't worry about the Muppets; they'll be all right.
Wish I could do Bert and Ernie again
standing right there beside you.
But I know that I'll be in your dreams tonight,
and we'll do it all over again.
We'll do all those Muppet movies again,
so turn out the light and close your eyes.

I'm already there.
Don't make a sound.
I'm the Muppet movies you watch.
I'm Big Bird's feet.
I'm the whisper in the wind
and I'll be there until the end.
Can you feel the love that we share?

Oh, I'm already there.

We may be a thousand miles apart,
but I'll be with you wherever you are.
I'm already there.
Take a look around.
I'm the sunshine in Ernie's hair.
I'm Bert's paper clips.
I'm the whisper in the wind,
and I'll be there until the end.
Can you feel the love that we share?

Oh, I'm already there.
Oh, I'm already there.
Then Jim Henson closes his eyes.

Jim Henson
September 24, 1936 - May 16, 1990

Cupcakes: My Version

(Jennifer's fanfiction version adapted from "My Little Pony: Friendship is Magic" produced by Studio B Productions in October 2010.)

It was a beautiful day in Ponyville. All of the ponies had somewhere to be and Rainbow Dash was just flying through the clouds, happy as she pleases.

Then she almost forgot she had to meet Pinkie Pie at Sugarcube Corner in fifteen minutes. She thought about not going, but knowing Pinkie, she would be so sad and not happy.

So then she kicked into high gear and found Pinkie Pie jumping up and down.

"Hey, Rainbow Dash. I'm so glad you're here. We are going to have sooo much fun," said Pinkie Pie.

"So are we going to do some pranks or maybe some flying tricks I should try?" asked Rainbow Dash.

"Well, we could do that, but I was thinking we could make some cupcakes," said Pinkie Pie.

"Cupcakes? I don't know, Pinkie. I can't bake. Remember last time?" asked Rainbow Dash.

"Oh don't worry, Dash. I'll be doing most of the work and it will be so much fun," said Pinkie Pie with a smile.

"Okay, Pinkie. Let's go then," said Rainbow Dash.

"Good! Let's get started. First eat this cupcake," said Pinkie Pie.

"Wait a minute. I thought we were making cupcakes," said Rainbow Dash.

"Well, yes, we are. But I made this cupcake just

for you to taste test," said Pinkie Pie.

"Okay, Pinkie. I'll do it. Just give me the cupcake," said Rainbow Dash.

"All right. Here, take the cupcake," said Pinkie Pie. Then Rainbow Dash ate the cupcake and started to feel a little tired and then went to sleep. When Rainbow Dash woke up, she found herself tied to a chair and saw the room was filled with cobwebs and spiders, all over on the wall. Ponies were dangling from the ceiling, blood was dripping on the floor. Dash wanted to scream, but couldn't because she was so scared.

"Pinkie, what is going on here?" asked Rainbow Dash.

"Well, remember the zombie ponies and how some people think they're not real. Guess what? They are real and they want you," said Pinkie Pie.

As zombie ponies came closer and closer, they said, "Happy Birthday Rainbow Dash!"

"Happy Birthday? You mean it's my birthday? But what about the cobwebs and spiders?" asked Rainbow Dash.

"Oh, don't worry; they're fake," said Pinkie Pie.

"Okay. What about the ponies that are dangling from the ceiling with blood that was dripping on the floor?" asked Rainbow Dash.

"They're stuffed and filled with cherry soda," said Pinkie Pie.

"What about zombie ponies? They are real, right?" asked Rainbow Dash.

"Oh no. They're not real. They are just our friends," said Pinkie Pie.

"Yeah, it was the only way to get the party ready in time," said Apple Jack.

"We didn't want to tell you, so I made a spell on the cupcake so that you would fall asleep," said Twilight Sparkle.

"It was my idea to make the costume," said Rarity.

"I hope we didn't scare you too badly," said Fluttershy.

"Scared me? No. Well... maybe a little bit," said Rainbow Dash.

"We have a surprise for you," said Pinkie Pie.

"A surprise? Cool! What is it?" asked Rainbow Dash.

Just then the Wonderbolts came in, and Rainbow Dash was shocked to see Spitfire standing before her.

"So I hear it is your birthday today, right?" asked Spitfire.

"Um...yes. It is my birthday, but what are you doing here?" asked Rainbow Dash.

Then Spitfire handed Rainbow Dash a present and it was a Wonderbolt outfit.

"Really? You mean I am a Wonderbolt? Yes! I knew it. I am sooo happy!" said Rainbow Dash.

Rainbow Dash was so happy and enjoyed the party. There were games and cake. Rainbow Dash had a good time and she was finally a Wonderbolt.

The End

The Rainbow Factory (good ending)

(Jennifer's fanfiction version adapted from Aurora Dawn's short story,
" The Rainbow Factory" published in August 2011.)

As Scootaloo was chained up, she saw Rainbow Dash was staring at her.

" Well now, Scootaloo, any last words before I make a rainbow out of you?" asked Rainbow Dash.

" Yes, how can you do this, Rainbow? This isn't like you at all—the Rainbow Dash I know would never do this! Please don't do this! I-I-I love you," said Scootaloo, with tears in her eyes.

Rainbow Dash looked shocked. How could this happen? She would never do this to her friends—not even to Scootaloo.

" I'm so sorry, Scootaloo! I don't know what came over me. I was the fastest Pegasus in Cloudsdale and now I am a monster! Can you ever forgive me, Scootaloo?" asked Rainbow Dash.

" Yes, I forgive you. Now, can you do me a big favor and get me out of this thing before I become a rainbow, please?" asked Scootaloo.

" Sure thing, kid," said Rainbow Dash.

But as soon Rainbow Dash got Scootaloo free, she saw Dr. Atmosphere standing right there in front of her.

" Well, it looks like some pony doesn't want to do her job! Well, it's like the old saying: ' If you want something done right, you have to do it yourself,'" said Dr. Atmosphere.

" NO! I won't let you turn Scootaloo into a

rainbow," shouted Rainbow Dash.

As soon as Dr. Atmosphere heard that, he ran after them. But as he was running, he slipped on a banana peel and fell right into the machine. Out came the most beautiful rainbow and he was nowhere to be seen.

"Wow! That was cool! So, Rainbow Dash, what do you want to do now?" asked Scootaloo.

"Well, how about we get out of here and I will teach you to fly the right way," said Rainbow Dash.

"Okay, Rainbow Dash, but what about the factory? Who is going to own it now?" asked Scootaloo.

Before Rainbow Dash could answer, there was a knock at the door and Rainbow Dash opened it. There stood a mysterious figure dressed in all black with only a mane and tail showing, which were pink.

"I'll be happy to take the factory off your hooves," said the mysterious figure.

"Oh, okay, thanks! Here are the keys to the factory—have fun," said Rainbow Dash.

Just as Rainbow Dash and Scootaloo walked out of the factory, they could hear an evil laugh inside the factory. They ran for their lives. Before long, the Rainbow Factory was changed into the Cupcake Factory.

The End?

Resources

CHARGE Syndrome Foundation: www.chargesyndrome.org

CHARGE Syndrome Geneticist, Meg Hefner, MS, Genetic Counselor, Associate Professor, Saint Louis University, Special Advisor, CHARGE Syndrome Foundation: meg@chargesyndrome.org

CHARGE Syndrome Geneticist: Donna Martin, donnamm@umich.edu

Pulmonary Hypertension Association: www.phassociation.org

NORD (National Organization for Rare Disorders): www.rarediseases.org

United States Department of Health and Human Services: www.hhs.gov

Office of Special Education Programs-U.S. Department of Education: www.ed.gov/about/offices/list/osers/osep

U.S. Department of Education, Office of Special Education Programs: idea.ed.gov/explore/home

Horseback riding (PATH International): www.pathintl.org

Therapy Dogs Inc.: www.therapydogs.com

Make-A-Wish Foundation: www.wish.org

Make-A-Wish Foundation of Michigan: wishmich.org

The Arc, For Children and Adults with Intellectual and Developmental Disabilities: www.thearc.org

The Arc of Northwest Wayne County-Michigan: www.thearcnw.org

Programs to Educate All Cyclists: bikeprogram.org

Michigan Adaptive Sports: michiganadaptivesports.org

Detroit Puppeteers Guild: www.detroitpuppeteersguild.org

Author

Carolyn Siewicki wanted to honor her daughter, Jennifer, by writing about her amazing life. She wants Jennifer's story to inspire all people, ease their burdens, and offer up peace, faith, and motivation in everyday living.

Carolyn has been a Special Education Paraprofessional for the past eighteen years. Carolyn worked at General Motors for seven years before starting a family. She has three children, Matthew, Christopher, and Jennifer, two daughters-in-law, Shera and Gemina, and six beautiful grandchildren: Devin, Anna, Lauren, Austin, Dylan, and Alexandra. Her mother, Olga, and brother, Gary, are also a big part of her life. In her free time, she enjoys spending time with her family and friends, motorcycle riding, gardening, and the outdoors. Carolyn resides in southeastern Michigan with her husband, Larry, daughter, Jennifer, and dog, Cindy.

Please visit Carolyn at carolynsiewickibooks.com.

"I first met Jennifer when she was twenty-eight years old. She is an inspiring young woman who has overcome many obstacles. This book is a testament to her spirit, courage, and compassion."
~Dr. Donna M. Martin, MD, PhD, Associate Professor, the University of Michigan Departments of Pediatrics and Human Genetics

"*The Joys of Jennifer* is a very poignant story that tugs at the reader's heart. It is an incredible testimony of the Siewickis' love for their daughter, Jennifer, and their faith in God. An uplifting story for anyone to read, especially parents of children with special needs."
~Jane Thompson, Oakland University OPTIONS Manager

"Carolyn Siewicki's memoir, *The Joys of Jennifer*, is a beautifully written dedication to her daughter. This inspirational story is about the abilities of a medically challenged young lady who has overcome many obstacles in her life. The dedication, encouragement, and support of her positive family have helped the high-spirited Jennifer achieve many goals and accomplishments."
~Melissa Shaw, Special Education Teacher

"If anything can be taken away from this story it is the boundless love of parents, the grace of God, and the indomitable strength within Jennifer."
~Annette Pellegrini, Special Education Paraprofessional

"This is a very inspirational story and reconfirms that with dedication, determination, and love all things are possible."
~Bev Lipmyer, Pulmonary Hypertension Patient